Life with a Passion

a Journey of Discovery

Travel into an awakening.

Discover life empowerment.

by

Sonja Onthank

InsiteRose Publishing

Portland, Oregon

www.lifewithapassion.com

Onthank, Sonja

Life with a Passion, *a Journey of Discovery*

Subjects Covered: 1) Self Actualization, 2) Self Esteem, 3) Effective Communication, 4) Depression, and 5) Financial Mastery.

Edition Description: *Life with a Passion* provides the supportive framework of a Life Empowerment Makeover®. The author blends real life stories to invoke dialogue about life transformation principles.

ISBN: 0-9778112-0-4 $14.95 (USD)

Published Edition: v2.1557

© Copyright 2006-2007 by Sonja Onthank

® Trademarks of InsiteRose Publishing pending

Photographs by Sonja Onthank *(www.lifewithapassion.com)*

Cover artwork by Slanted Styles Design *(www.slantedstyles.com)*

Printed in the United States of America

Published and Distributed by:

> InsiteRose Publishing
> P.O. Box 23843
> Portland, OR 97281 - USA
> 1.503.624.7282
> Email: insiterose@yahoo.com

Table of Contents

In Memory of...

Edward Noel and Hans Dietrich

In Appreciation of...

My heartfelt appreciation is extended to family, friends, counselors, editors and designers who contributed to this project. They provided many wonderful suggestions that I am grateful to have received. Thankful for this support, I share this gift for the world to enjoy.

Preface

This journey explores traditional values and modern-day life. We span across common concerns affecting millions of people to assess how dreams intensify as a deeper understanding of willpower unfolds. We discuss love, justice, power and liberty, as this propels passion. Passion has a strong liking for certain activities. We will explore passion interactively as we travel into a journey of discovery.

Folks from all walks of life had a chance to provide feedback to this content. I was fascinated to see how it compelled them to take action on their goals. This sparked a need for me to invest more time and money to make *Life with a Passion* a physical reality for everyone to enjoy. I share this news, because it is invigorating, inspiring and incredibly powerful. *Life with a Passion* started after my nephews and nieces experienced the loss of their father's life. I was heart-stricken with grief to have lost my brother, and I wanted to do something special for his kids. I looked for a gift that focused on long-term happiness. I wanted a guide that covered a vast number universal challenges that we are all likely to face. My goal was to have an orientation that explains how to attain success. Many books covered a topic like rekindling love relationships or dealing with grief acceptance. Some books had celebrities illustrating fantastic achievements. At times I felt distanced from a fame-oriented viewpoint or a single topic. I decided to record my findings wherein one hundred books were used. These are referenced in the Bibliography. I compiled this content into a fast-paced solution, and I'm very pleased to know that you have an opportunity to participate. This book may confirm what you already know or it might affirm what you want to believe. Most importantly, it is designed to create conversations about life experiences with your friends and family.

My mission took three years to develop. Every day I dedicated time to articulate the essence of passion. It was an ardent effort. I decided to liven the presentation with some poetry and a bit of humor. I anticipate that you have many priorities, so I've attempted to save you time by introducing life's most crucial concerns. Additionally, most people have a limited financial budget. Although exorbitant wealth is enjoyed by two percent of the population, the ticket for happiness is reasonable prosperity. There are plenty of "how-to get rich" schemes, but I've focused on resourceful way to address this topic—it is based on how much you earn today. Passion is a quest to improve time and money utilization.

Between seven chapters are famous quotes and beautiful photographs that remind me of great achievements. When given the right tools, time and skill, success can emerge. Success requires an enormous amount of dedication, effort and planning. We have a roadmap for this preparation, and that is called the **Life Empowerment Makeover**®. This progressively leads to a self actualization formula, which is an inward journey to understand goals and thought-provoking spiritual concepts without questioning religious dogma. Life devotions may answer the fabled-old questions of: Who are you? And, what do you want to become? I take it a step further by explaining what one might expect when they get there. I do this without providing all the answers; rather I provide many questions to ponder. The plot for this odyssey is to help you thrive and prosper.

– Sonja Onthank

How to Use This Book

(1) The delta symbol (**Δ**) refers to pages in the back of the book. This is also referred to as the **Life Empowerment Makeover**®. If you don't want to write in this book, a separate reprint of the Appendix may be ordered. With the exception of the Cultural Portrait and Personal Billboard exercises, most assignments take about ten minutes to complete.

(2) This book is written using "you" and "we" interchangeably. Occasionally "he" or a "she" is used but both genders are referenced neutrally.

(3) Photographs were taken by the author at the following sites: Schloss Lugwigslust, Schloss Sanssouci (Potsdam/Berlin), Schloss Moritzburg, Schloss Pillnitz (Dresden), and the beautiful baroque gardens of Saxony.

(4) Specific quotes were limited to one or two sentences to preserve copyrights. The bibliography was limited to one book per author.

(5) There are ongoing tools such as **Life Tracker**®, **Organizational Journal**, **Weekly Intentions**®, **Finance Tracker**® and the **Life Empowerment Makeover**®. The website www.lifewithapassion.com has more information about these products.

(6) You have an opportunity to contribute to the overall effectiveness of this program by providing personal feedback and sharing "**Career Insights**" commentary to: author@lifewithapassion.com. If you wish to send us a letter, the address is: InsiteRose Publishing, PO Box 23843, Portland OR 97281.

(7) If you are interested becoming a life coach, please contact us to get information about the *License for Passion* training kit.

A Toast for Life with a Passion

Trust the process without seeking control

Take things as they come and expect no more

Seek companionship that makes you laugh

Find abundance in things you craft

Rejoice in music with great satisfaction

Experience Life with a Passion.

Chapter One: Getting to Know You

Cultural Dispositions

A birthplace marks an origin of start
Inheriting traits that make you smart
Motivating yearnings for the heart
Life with a Passion creates assurance
That you have a tremendous endurance
Seeking knowledge and perseverance.

Our adventure starts with a look at genetic hardwiring and personality traits. This probes into an explanation of the paradoxical aspects to life, where there is a willingness to accept challenge while at the same time hope for triumph. Similar to a slumber that gets jolted into reality as one falls out of bed, *Life with a Passion* is an awakening for dreams to come alive. This surprising arousal will look at challenges (which are often predictable) and assess triumph (this is less predictable). Humans are programmed to avoid calamities and face challenges to achieve success. We'll uncover topics related to success, which is defined as being able to create intellectual property without fear of condemnation by self or others.

I hope to inspire an awakening. I'd like to see you make a wish for something exciting and invigorating. You might wish for a vacation, so you can go to an exotic place that you've never experienced before. Imagine for a moment that you are on a vacation right now... Enjoy the beautiful pictures that were captured when solitude was felt. Considered the lives of past generations and the struggles they had to endure. Discover future paths to venture upon as the secret for happiness is hidden somewhere on this expeditious adventure. You might meditate for a moment. You might participate in an exercise that enlightens you. You might witness a theatrical performance and feel your soul resonates with a life blessing. Fill your imagination with courage, while a metamorphosis attempts to stimulate a greater belief in self.

This journey is a realization, a glimmering hope for personal success. You ponder on extraordinary things to accomplish, such as developing a career goal, pursuing a thrill and seeking more satisfaction with day-to-day life. You might want to help someone with his or her marvelous goal. You might be interested in playing a musical instrument, being in theatrics or skydiving. We look at empowerment, so extraordinary pursuits can be a reality. My plan ensures that there is a focus to serve the needs of a family and self. I accepted a personal dare to let my extraordinary activity be a work of creation. The **Life Empowerment Makeover**® was the result of my burning desire. Here in the Land of Opportunity astounding possibilities exist. A black and white sketch of my life has color added, and this vibrant story shows how dreams become a reality. My dream to write in an appealing manner was a personal dare to be studious and tenacious. This passion was realized after a lot of ardent effort, but hopefully it gives you a possibility to help others find purpose in their life. We might have some crossover similarities to our motivating strides. A cultural portrait will pinpoint if this is the case. It is a description of one's calling in life.

Cultural Portrait

Life stories demonstrate risks taken and bold transformations made. They also reveal how habits were formed during childhood and adulthood. With a cultural portrait, these twenty questions are answered:

1. As a child, what did you want to be?

2. What character traits did you learn from your parents?

3. What came effortlessly for you during your youth?

4. What playful activities did you enjoy the most?

5. What are you drawn to do (arts, craft, dance, sports)?

6. What do you want to learn?

7. Describe your favorite mentor or President?

8. Did you excel at certain subjects in school?

9. How do you participate with music or theater now?

10. What do you choose to do for entertainment?

11. What are your most prominent career experiences?

12. How do you participate with your community?

13. What are your key travel experiences like?

14. Who are your best friends and what are they like?

15. What is it like to have dinner at home?

16. What do you do on a typical family vacation?

17. How is discipline established in your family?

18. How would you describe the holiday season?

19. How are chores handled for each person in your family?

20. How would you describe your ethnic identity?

These questions describe life at home, in school and on the job. Your cultural portrait gets you to think, "Oh, so that's where I got that from," if you have interviewed your parents with these questions. Your natural gifts are discovered when you look at the guardian source. Cultural portraits reach a prudent conclusion, called a life credo. Ask this question to find a credo:

"Based on life experiences, what resonates as your favorite slogan or credo that you live by?"

My cultural portrait is below. This is a chronological perspective of the major life transformations that have occurred for my parents and self. This demonstrates how a cultural portrait is written. Writing a portrait is time consuming, but rewarding. You'll see **bold font** ending each paragraph. Those statements were completed well after the story was written. It is the summation I identified as a family value (a learning experience from each transition or paragraph). Those bold statements can lead to an epiphany about yourself, which we will cover later. A cultural portrait is a fun way to get to know someone completely:

My father's life started on Christmas Eve in 1934 in British Guyana, a small country situated on the northern coast of South America that has a lush rainforest that occupies nearly half the country's land. Colonized by the United Kingdom, this tropical country has a diverse culture representing six ethnic groups—Africans, Carib Amerindian tribes, Chinese, East Indians, Europeans and Portuguese. My father's "Guyanese" roots came mostly from the Caribbean island of Barbados. He was the eldest of ten children, making him old enough to have joined his father on explorations into the interior mainland of the dense Amazon rainforest. His father guided diamond miners into the jungle. Here faint streams of light pass through swamps as plants grow endlessly into tall coconut trees and exotic wildwoods. Ocelots, crocodiles, anteaters, monkeys, brilliantly colored birds and venomous snakes fill the landscape of this humid climate. My father's dreams at night were filled with a remarkable sense of invincibility. **Take some risk, explore the world and enjoy the magnitude of Mother Nature's grandeur.**

His father became a bookkeeper as the years progressed and when more children arrived. My papa was the mentor for his siblings. He attended school, graduating with top honors. This granted him the unique opportunity to attend a university abroad. This privilege was extended to only ten students in the country. He went to the University of Edinburgh during the late 1950's where he met my mother. In Scotland, he had his first child, Hans Dietrich. A year later my second brother, Rainer Russell, was born in Germany. The family went to Guyana so he could fulfill a work-contract that would repay the scholarship he obtained. He utilized his eco-science education for the next seven years as two additional children were born, Fiona and myself, Sonja. **Education is a privilege extended to most everyone, even when the odds are 1 in 100,000 people!**

Guyana's Ministry of Forestry hired him to supervise a small crew to catalogue the contents of the rainforest. They used a heavy chain to measure a thirty-three square foot area of land so they could survey the jungle on a micro level. This kept his inquisitive nature alive. When he returned to the community, he had fascinating stories to tell. He was able to keep everyone spellbound for hours as he vibrantly described a life similar to Tarzan of the Jungle. There was humor and excitement in these adventurous tales. For example, he once mistook a giant anaconda as a log to sit on. This resting place soon turned into a shocking realization that he had to run as fast as he could. He illustrated what it would be like if this snake wrapped him into fatal suffocation. He gestured the exhaustive race for survival, dramatizing this with eye-popping captivation. Perhaps this snake did whip around and face him eye-to-eye to assess if he could be swallowed in one gulp. Was he a worthwhile snack or vice versa? He had an innate ability to repeat the many sounds animals make and he fully understood the freeze, fight or flight instinct of danger. The most dangerous predator, however, was a tiny mosquito likely to transmit diseases, such as malaria—which once he self-cured by lying on a rock for days in the blazing tropical sun. He spoke of living off the land, eating a flour bake strapped to his waist, juxtaposing to a machete that would slash their way through the bush. In the pursuit of science he discovered a brotherhood that stems from courage. **Courage is not the absence of fear—it is a resilience to survive harsh environments, where one expects potential risks.**

In 1968 we came to America. His first job was well outside his engineering abilities, but he quickly became an expert. Only four years later he started a business called North American Controls. This company manufactured large sawmill equipment. He visited sawmills and took hundreds of pictures to assess how modern equipment would be installed to optimize lumber production. This was when he coined the expression, "If it wasn't for the last minute, I wouldn't get anything done." During the 1970s, he was on the leading edge of computer technology. He drafted architectural plans and plotted monumental equipment designs with 80 highly skilled employees. Over the next decade, Papa flourished and his role of authority was well matched to his magnetizing personality and incredible work ethic. He had a rather brassy personality at times. For example, when I called him at work his retort might be, "Call me back. I'm in the midst of a ping-pong game with a client that I intend to cream, even if that means losing the million dollar contract I've just proposed." In addition to his funny nature and entrepreneurial spirit, he had enormous wisdom and perspective. **Opportunity is a matter of hard-earned sweat equity, and having the wisdom to be in the right place and the right time with the proper skills to utilize talents.**

Papa always challenged his children to do their best with his hallmark song, "Anything you can do, I can do better." This not only led us to getting him to do all sorts of antics like reciting Shakespeare or doing gymnastic maneuvers, but it also taught us an invaluable lesson to do our very best. Even when we brought home straight A's on a report card, it wasn't good enough for him. He quizzed us to see if we had the intellectual acumen to pass a grade according to his expectations of what we should know. Papa himself never lost his love for learning. **Keep yourself challenged; the quest for knowledge is an experience that extends well beyond schooling, it comes from curiosity.**

He was self-taught to a large extend, even when it came to speaking foreign languages fluently. He had a jovial personality and a bold presence with unforgettable luminosity. His personal credo was **to live each day, as if it were his last.**

My mother's life is so diametrically different from my father's that even her birthday of April's Fools Day seems ironic to Christmas Eve. She was brought up prim and proper in a manor situated in eastern Germany. Her family once had an aristocratic status in the heart of three farming villages, where crop harvests and hunting lodges were part of a provincial structure that was quickly changing. In a small village, south of Berlin, there stood a central church and train station which anchored the extent of a social life my mother experienced. She attended a single room school and learned from rote memorization assignments that were doled out for each grade level by a single teacher for all ages. My mother and her brother were prodigies in this school environment. They would be the only kids who would later attend a finishing school as secondary education. Her family upbringing required top-notch manners, using proper etiquette and social graces at all times. **Manners are universal—they reflect a status in life.**

Her father was bed-ridden during most of her youth. He had an illness that could be treated with Penicillin today, but at that time it was the cause of his premature death. Her mother, to whom I call Oma, (this is the German word for grandmother) was the master of the home. Oma had to put on pretense that she "consulted with her husband" while her husband was very sick. During World War II, grandfather died. This was during a time that my mother knitted socks and mittens for the Germany army. She attended youth programs designed to teach national pride. Their little castle had several POW residents who remained after the First World War, as they were an integral part of the household. Naturally her home was a prime target for WWII army invasion. Horrible nightmares preceded the arrival of Russian foot soldiers. Many atrocities occurred thereafter. These memories are just too painful for my mother to retell. While soldiers occupied their home, there was one moment to escape. The Russian POW (who was their chauffer and gardener) risked his own life to help them flee. As military occupants slept, he untied the shackles. After the family escaped, they saw their small castle engulfed in flames just moments later. Oma and her two children were completely impoverished as they boarded the last train out of Berlin before the Iron Curtain fell. **One can lose everything when greed or terrorism is close at hand.**

My mother attended a boarding school specifically for displaced war civilians in West Germany. While buildings, roads and markets were in complete shambles, her diet consisted mostly of boiled potatoes and cabbage. Clothing was made from old country flags that no longer resembled a nationality. Outgrowing shoes was a burden to bear. Education was vital. If she failed one class or received more than two C grades, it would result in expulsion—and that meant homelessness.

She learned the usual subjects such as French, Latin, and English with strict discipline. This created an opportunity for her to be a valued asset outside her native country only a few years later. She went to Switzerland to be a nanny where she spoke French. She moved to Belgium to work as a language translation secretary, where she took shorthand in one language and translated it to German. The Cold War promoted a great need for her language skills. **Talents are developed when a skill is practiced and utilized repeatedly.**

She met my father while attending a music festival in Scotland. After the marriage, she voyaged across the Atlantic Ocean to live in the tropics for seven years. She experienced many cultural migrations thus far, but Guyana was truly the most radical shift imaginable. Now she enjoyed spicy conversations that collided with other people talking. Mutti is the German word for mother and that's what everyone calls her. She started a bag factory that consisted of women bringing their own sewing machines to the site using materials she outsourced. We lived at grandmother's house at this time. There were two other grandchildren living with grandmother, my cousins whose mother lived in England. These cousins were of similar age to my older brothers. Grandmother didn't like the responsibility of yet another youngster (me) at home. Mutti was told it was compulsory for me to move across town to live with my Godmother and she had little authority to contest this decision. The move to America created hope for personal freedom. **Keep families intact—even temporary separations can alter a sense of self-assurance for children.**

When we arrived in the United States, Mutti feared that her English was still prone to improper pronunciation or verb usage (after all this was not her native language). She spoke English for the past seven years while living in the tropics, but she was truly shocked to get honorary acceptance of a two-year college equivalency after taking an entrance exam. Quickly she earned a Bachelor's Degree and she applied this to a career. She was a Corporate Recruiter (this was called "a Headhunter" back then—hardly a politically correct term by today's standards). She worked full-time, which was a bit unusual for women during the 1970's. She did not fear what she didn't know, and she did all things well. Fortunately this was a time for women's liberation so she flourished in a professional recruiting career. **A career is a valuable asset, well primed with an objective and continued education.**

Mutti enjoys cultural events, foreign film, museum exhibits and world news. She maintains a lovely garden with utmost tenacity. She has steadfast determination and offers honest feedback, from a pragmatic viewpoint. Her mission is **to leave a legacy for future generations to enjoy.**

I was born in Guyana while a drastic economic downfall occurred in the early 1960's. A self-governed parliament was forming and that led to civil riots. There was a full-on economic strike, which meant gasoline and electricity was not available. My mother was taken to the hospital on a bicycle in the midst of a hot summer day! Gradually the economic situation stabilized, but we ventured to America after my fifth birthday. We started life here with a few family heirlooms, mostly Caribbean decorations. Our trunk of clothes quickly acclimated to a new wardrobe of tennis shoes and gym shorts. Our home was situated in a suburb of Portland Oregon, where expansive yards wrap around towering fir trees. Impressive mountains, tall buildings and huge parking lots seemed to contribute to the bigness of America. My mother actually came home with hundreds of grocery items, conveniently tucked into the trunk of a car. Amazing inventions were everywhere. Becoming American citizen instilled an important value to believe in national pride. **Be proud of your humble beginnings.**

As a child, I played outside constantly. My brothers, sister and I would swing from a long rope from the tallest tree, jumping off the fence to swing back and forward. Our star-trek reenactments were equipped with handmade forts built without parental supervision. We rode bikes everywhere—even in the pouring rain! We made handcrafted gifts during the holidays, and our favorite gift exchange was the brown paper wrapped carton sent from Oma. Life was festive, creative and easy going. We rarely saw our relatives—apart from the occasional visitor that felt as if a dignitary person was in our presence. My childhood consisted of pleasant weather, wrestling with my brothers, singing songs and dancing to lively calypso or rock music. **Celebrate life with art, dance and music.**

I received tremendous guidance from my lovely sister, Fiona. Although I'm accused of following her around like a puppy dog back then as a mere youngster, she remains my best friend. We routinely visited elderly couples in the neighborhood, as this was a Girl Scout duty that turned into a habit. They really appreciated our companionship, especially after a spouse died. Quite often they were completely alone for months at a time, except for the visits from us. The song Eleanor Rigby (by The Beatles) reminded me of them. Later, I joined a Pathfinder group because it was coed which suited my preference better. **Be of service to your community—interact with people who are lonely, pick up litter and be helpful whenever possible.**

When I was twelve, my parents settled on a divorce rather quickly. Suddenly the family was completely dismantled. It didn't take long for my father to establish another family elsewhere. My oldest brother was given a scholarship to attend Columbia University. My second brother pursued chess tournaments across the nation. My sister went to France, after attending a nursing school in New York City. I was a latchkey teenager with too much time on my hands. I filled this lonely void with an adolescent boyfriend, and a pregnancy came about. This romance abruptly ended in physical abuse, as I was sleeping one night. He barged into the house in a drunken state with needless anger. I dedicated the remaining years of my life to be the best mother possible, but this started when I was only seventeen years old. **I cannot depend on others to support me.**

After four months of secretarial training, my first job was at a non-profit agency that specialized in elderly neglect, family counseling and a foster grandparent program. Using carbon paper and goopy whiteout, I masked many typos. It was blatantly obvious that I had a negligible high school education from the frequency in which I relied on this goop. I enrolled in community college classes while working full-time for the next five years. During that time I was an office assistant with an architectural firm working on the twenty-year plan for our local zoo, and then I was a Pension Assistant for a large Fortune 100 company. This was when my life goals changed. I typed annual earning reports for chief executive officers while at the same time I processed a pension settlement for a person who worked 45 years at a lumber plant. I saw a huge disparity of wealth causing me to realize that I needed a retirement plan. The president of this company was a maverick in the business world and he inspired me. **Find your passion, enhance your skills, and do what resonates in your heart.**

I accepted the position of an International Sales Manager with a software company. This role made it possible for me to travel to twenty countries repeatedly. I was away from home for twelve to sixteen weeks at a time. I was usually training new employees or providing sales presentations. I had an important role to fill until the job market plummeted at the turn of the new millennium. A few years later I was selling leadership curriculum for teens. One morning I got the grim news that my brother died. Upon returning from his funeral, I started writing this book. He started a charter school called Advanced College and his legacy was related to Philosophy, in particular where the works of Shakespeare would be compared with modern Disney movies. In the wake of this loss, I have given people a chance to compare and contrast my migratory and modern life. I made this gift for my daughter, my two lovely grandchildren and my brother's kids in his honor. **Quality parenting brings long-term happiness—especially when future generations gain intellectual knowledge from past generations.**

I am tenacious and I have a conscientious nature. My personal credo is **to appreciate what I have and live life with a passion.**

You'll notice exercises are placed in the Appendix, which is called the **Life Empowerment Makeover**®. Here you can jot down the family credo statements. When you feel like taking a break from reading, just conduct an exercise at the back of the book. This first assignment is to write the credo, but you might want to write cultural portraits as well.

Δ Exercise 1: Family Credo—Life Mission (pages 122)

My cultural portrait revealed that I felt uneasy about getting support from others. This principle came about when I married the wrong guy at a young age. I allowed myself to not expect support from others. For many years this was the case. Suddenly the word "collaboration" popped in my mind while I was reflecting on this. This coincided with another family value to be of service to my community. If I changed my viewpoint about people supporting each other, then I could invite more support into my life. I authenticated this belief by embracing a new thought to enhance my communication with others. The other thing I discovered about my portrait was the affect of a family separation. Many wonderful aspects of character strengths were determined by this exercise. Now we will look at personality traits as our next topic.

Dispositions

How you communicate will most likely be a disposition. There is quiz to cover the top ten dispositions. Although this is not a scientific theory to reach definitive conclusions, it is a fun quiz that incorporates several personality profiling systems. Please, get a pen or pencil to complete each question with your first instinctive response. There are three possible answers: **No, Maybe (or Sometimes) and Yes**. Circle questions that make you think, "Yeah, but I'm working on that one," or, "Doesn't everyone?" If you hesitate for a moment, circle that question as well. Circled questions may be profound—it could relate to a communicative trait you want to consider later. Attempt to answer all the statements with *Yes* or *No* as often as possible.

Δ Exercise 2: Disposition Quiz (page 123-124)

If you answer *No* to most of the questions in a section, you probably possess the trait listed at the top. If you answer **Yes** in most cases, you likely possess the trait listed at the bottom of each section. If you have an equal number of **Yes** and **No** or **Maybe** answers for a category, then it is **neutral** trait. Omit neutral traits from your final conclusion—for example, my disposition is a communicative, assertive, creative and unstructured disposition. Here are the traits used for the quiz:

No: Passive, Assertive, Pragmatic, Introvert or Disciplined

Yes: Communicative, Aggressive, Creative, Extrovert or Unstructured.

Communicative, Passive, Assertive or Aggressive dispositions are likely to be life-long personality traits. **Creative, Pragmatic, Extroverted, Introverted, Disciplined or Unstructured traits** are likely influenced from social environments that change as interests shift from one to another. For example, if you enroll in an art class, your disposition may be oriented to unstructured traits where you attempt to think outside the box. If you work for a highly structured company, you are probably more disciplined and timely. You might find it helpful to consider these dispositions during confrontations or frustrations. You'll probably deal with challenge successfully when you match your disposition to that of the other person. For example, if you are talking with someone who has a passive disposition, you might ask a question that enables them to speak for others rather than stating an opinion for oneself.

Passive people avoid conflicts, usually stating an opinion after the fact or when it is relevant to do so. They are generally reserved about sharing their feelings. They like to think of a peace-seeking mission and they favor the underdog in a group setting. They are happy to contribute to a common mission, but they might resist offering suggestions.

Communicative persons confront problems as they occur. They are compelled to help others respond to situations, regardless of the difficulty. They can be extremely sensitive to other people's feelings, and they like getting input from everyone involved. They make suggestions whenever possible. They are good at solving difficult problems.

Assertive personalities state their opinion fearlessly. They have a great sense of willingness to find solutions. They seek effectiveness and logical reasoning. They express their needs directly and they are open to multiple outcomes. They usually want people to participate freely. They are good at coaching others to be independent.

Aggressive people guard their point of view; usually hoping others will agree. They avoid elusive situations and find it frustrating to deal with ambiguity. They are go-getters, usually expecting a specific outcome when projects start. They don't mind risk. They hope everyone readily accepts a project and they prefer to lead decisions.

Pragmatic personalities practice reasoning and logic. They may need functionality in things rather than artistic expressiveness because sensible explanations are often preferred. They look for an easy fix or practical solution. Rather than seeking a variety of options, they seek a black and white answer.

Creative people are expressive with what-if scenarios. They don't mind if the situation is complex or has multiple outcomes. They are inspired to recommend brilliant ideas and they often invent creative solutions. They are usually verbose when given the chance to express themselves.

Introverts might avoid group-oriented settings. They look for problem resolutions in a confidential environment. With individual roles clearly defined, the introvert will be at ease. They can be shy, and prefer to not volunteer feedback.

Extroverts courageously make recommendation and feel good when everyone works together with shared responsibilities. They are usually outspoken or they may not need a lot of prodding for an answer.

Disciplined persons favor routine, scheduled regimens. They may want a project clearly defined with detailed instructions, timelines and designated roles. They work well when there are milestones for a project and there is little change to the plan.

Unstructured individuals have a strong need for personal freedom. They like open-ended, spontaneous decisions. They might implement projects on a whim. They usually accept change willingly.

It is common to mimic a disposition while communicating. For example, a fast talker can cause you to respond rapidly. Disposition-matching happens all the time. To match the disposition of another person, you might talk about conceptual ideas rather than concrete facts. You might speak of a general time frame instead of a specific time. The next topic, the Public Eye Chart, relates to a broader perspective of character traits.

The Public Eye Chart

People you see frequently might be prone to offering feedback about your personality. This can be an instrumental aspect of developing self esteem, to which there are four aspects:

1. **What you know of yourself is consistent with how others view you.** (Subconsciously Aware: You project this personality to the outside world and it is a natural way for you to act, think or plan.)

2. **Habits you conceal.** (Consciously Aware: You are aware that you conceal these habits, because you adjust actions for the public eye's sake.)

3. **What you *do not* realize about your character.** (Consciously Unaware: You are unaware that a talent is in development, but others see a noticeable propensity for this skill.)

4.   **Talents to be developed with time and dedication.** (Subconsciously Unaware: You and the public do not realize certain skills and talents are yet to be pursued.)

American psychologists, _Jo_seph Luft and _Ha_rry _I_ngham, classified these four points as quadrants in the 1950's. This developed a theory called Johari's Windows. The quadrants are defined as: 1) the open arena, 2) the façade, 3) the unaware blind spot, and 4) the unknown. Each quadrant is diagrammed as a window that varies in size, depending on the person and public opinion. This examination of self is a means of viewing your actions from the lens of others. If you have a personal style openly revealed to the public, conscious actions are accepted as the style you want to project. The window of concealed habits is not organically the way you act. People accept a genuine aspect of style as it moves to the open arena. This is when the public feels sincere about who you are. When acceptance occurs, between you and the public, the possibility for passion emerges. On the flip side of this scenario, you might have been told that you exude certain strengthens that you didn't know existed.

The Public Eye Chart is a quiz that requires an extemporaneous answer from people listed atop the chart. Ask these folks to rank an instant response for each consecutive word on the list. Please complete the sentence, **"Am I _____?"** using the consecutive word on the list below with one of these answers: **0=never, 1=seldom, 2=occasionally, 3=mostly, 4=always.**

Δ Exercise 3: Public Eye Chart (page 125)

Are your answers consistent with the public eye? Did you agree with them? Are you concerned about a specific word on the chart? Were you fearful of judgments made by others? This confidence-building exercise is an opportunity to assess character traits. This chart looks your perspective and the public eye's viewpoint.

The swells of an ocean create a wonderful opportunity for surfing. A surfer rides a treacherous wave, even if the risk of sharks exists. Patience was required to get to the perfect wave. This demonstrates a breakthrough event to shout the words, "I can't take it anymore" or "This is great!" When a breaking point occurs, there can be potential success or failure. Sometimes a breaking point occurs after three to five weeks of starting a new school or job. A breaking point can occur when exhaustion kicks in. This comes from too much exposure or when a crossroad event creates compulsive action. A breaking point emotion may be felt when you complete this chart. Words on the Public Eye Chart might touch a nerve. You might have a hunch about something affecting your health, wealth or relationships. The question to ask might be: "What if a word on the Public Eye Chart is an issue for (someone)?" Or, "Is there a place where a word on the Public Eye Chart creates a breaking-point?" Precautionary measures to prevent catastrophic events require action on your part. Goal setting or character improvements may be directly related to a treacherous experience or extremely rewarding outcome.

Brainstorming

Brainstorming ideas are things you've always wanted to accomplish, but you might need the power of passion sprinkled into the equation. Our next assignment is a list of brainstorming questions. Attempt to answer the following questions where there are no restrictions—you have a surplus of skill, money and tools to do whatever you want to do.

Exercise 4: Brainstorming Questions

What activities make me happy? *(Professional interests, flying, golf, music, projects, sports, travel sites, etc.)*

Where do I like to go when I'm on vacation? *(Thrills, arenas, concerts, bookstores, theater, restaurants, parties, wildlife, parks)*

What would be the most enjoyable career for me?

What do I find particularly interesting to learn?

What kind of life do I truly want to have in the future?

What charities or political interests appeal to me?

I wish I could...

These questions have possibility-oriented conclusions. Passion is ignited by possibilities. Sometimes obstacles can prohibit brainstorming ideas, but we waver in and out of ambition modalities all the time. As we coast along in a comfort zone, this can ironically be a time when there is little inclination to pursue passion. At other times uncomfortable life circumstances cause us to work harder at developing a passion because it will resolve problems. As you look under the hood of ambition, you get to see brainstorming ideas can instill personal pride. The upcoming exercise is a discussion of virtues. This discussion will be the ingredients for pride. I've done a close study on motivating pride, and I found it is enriched by a virtue.

Discussion of Virtues

There are many virtues that come from proverbs in a Bible or from fortune cookie. A famous person may quote a virtue or it stems directly out of a cultural portrait. I'll ask you to think of a story for the virtues outlined. These twelve virtues will hopefully prompt a discussion if you read each one out loud. See if a particular virtue strikes a cord with your mission in life.

Exercise 5: Discussion of Virtues

Influence power with choice.

Power is not fueled with anger or animosity; power is choice. The irony of power is that you have it and then lose it. Power is the liberty to choose your destiny, even if a learning experience comes from trail and error.

Be a participant in this world.

As a citizen of a county, country and continent, you can campaign for a cause (such as preserving human dignity). Mother Teresa cared for lepers, even when everyone shunned these people, and now she is a legend. She's considered the most compassionate person of the century! The Golden Rule **"Do unto to others as you would have them do unto you"** might include that you love yourself as much as you love others.

Work hard. Be generous.

A community builds monuments to represent a culture of generosity. Notoriety comes from people who seek an endeavor to empower future generations and who hard work.

Stay curious and mentally stimulate the brain.

Knowledge is an ongoing quest to prevent mediocrity. Learning is a never-ending quest that becomes a great education. Investigate what you do not know to develop more skill. Talent emerges when a skill has been practiced.

The healthiest place to be is outside. Get physical.

The outdoor environment brings fresh air to your lungs and brain. Nature is an infinite light beyond our mere existence. The outdoor environment brings serenity that is experienced when you are on the path of awesome beauty and when you go to places to rejoice in the connection with the planet, you get to breathe the essence of creation.

> ## *Never apologize for your art.*

Art is the backbone of society—it inspires faith and a common good. Craft, poetry, gardening and music are easy gifts to make with little cost. Share your creative spirit, for it will connect your soul with creativity.

> ## *We all want respect from each another.*

Humans have become dispensable resources, as employers are likely to terminate jobs with little sense of loyal to the impact this change has on humans. We have one prevailing need and that is respect. If respect were to vanish, what would take its place—materialism?

> ## *Integrity. Integrity. Integrity.*

Integrity is the act of living with purpose, honesty and intention. Dishonest people rob the soul from companionship. Have you ever met a lair and found yourself uninterested in communicating with them? Humans need to trust that their communication is truthful and honored in a discreet manner.

> ## *Good manners are critical for success.*

Good manners are imperative. Etiquette is practiced in every day settings, not just at the dinner table. Social graces include offering a seat and asking if it's okay to state an opinion. You might find being courteous to every person you meet requires appropriate humor as well, where diversity is respected and individuality is acknowledged.

Embrace a positive attitude.

A cheerful disposition is always welcomed. Optimism is a cooperative spirit that can be infectious. A warm smile can be heard, even when you are on the phone. Vibrancy occurs when you speak proudly of others and of self. Embrace pride, for this is a sign that you are doing extraordinary activities and you invite passion into your life.

Stay out of trouble.

Jail may include three square meals a day, plus a cement block to sleep on, but the stigma stays with you like a tattoo that does not disappear. Go where there is little temptation for trouble to exist. Be with people who have no inclination for crime. Criminal influences can be infectious wherein one repeats their offensive ways until all power is lost.

Be accountable for your actions.

Keep promises to yourself—your authentic actions make life joyous.

Virtues might as well be bumper stickers on a car. They are a driving force behind goals. Virtues satisfy the soul with a burning desire to elevate what you are drawn to do. They align life principles to places you enjoy and people you want to meet. Even if resources are limited, the possibility of exploration is not. You learn to overcome life-inhibiting barriers, such as a lack of confidence or money, with professional coaches, contractors, counselors or organizers who attempt to get to know you. In order for them to help you, they will need to be aware of your virtues and life experiences. The final exercise is a questionnaire, which might be a useful tool in the process of getting to know you.

Δ Exercise 6: Self-Awareness (page 126-127)

When I walk past a large window and see a reflection that surprises me, such as a slumped posture, I immediately adjust my stance from a stoop to an upright and confident position. I call this "the Cinderella Syndrome." When I make an adjustment to what I expect the public eye to see, or when I get a glimpse of behavior that I was not cognizant of, Johari's Windows has proven that I am but a mere player in this vast world who can be open, fake, a work-in-process or potentially a great achiever. Cinderella is a fairytale that deals with a changed self image. This occurs after she makes an adjustment to her persona. Her tattered clothes embraced low self esteem. She experienced a life transformation after the power of passion intervened. This is an example of an empowerment breakthrough, wherein a person becomes aware of their greater potential.

A breakthrough transformation might be oriented to a clearly defined set of virtues. When virtues are in harmony with your sphere of influence (the public eye or people you see regularly), then your style is genuinely able to satisfy dreams. There are compelling reasons to have a dream, and that is to fulfill a virtue. Colossal achievement comes when personal pride is felt. Family values foster these virtues, but there are social experiences to influence virtues as well. One of my virtues came out of a scenario when I helped four teenage skiers who were stranded for the night. After this event, I felt enormous pride and I realized that we all want respect from each other.

This chapter gives a renewed sense of appreciation for good things in life. You traversed along the paths taken by ancestors and reviewed life philosophies from another person's perspective. You speculated how transformational events propel you to think of certain brainstorming ideas. This pinpoints people, places and events that have created your perspective. You found the source of pride, by considering extraordinary activities you have done. You saw how dispositions have different communication habits, which makes observing character traits more interesting. You started an empowerment process to create better outcomes for the future.

Love Equality

Nourish romance as a mutual need

For love is a treasured gift indeed

A radiant spirit with powerful grace

That bears no footprint on the face.

Chapter Two: Love Connections

Unequivocal Love.

"The love we have to give will be contingent upon the love we have experienced. But there is hope. Love is learned through loving."

~*Leo Buscaglia, author—Born for Love*

Friends help us acquire socialization skills. We hang out to express humor, laugh at our sentimental yearnings and learn to not take ourselves too seriously. Even though scruples are discussed with friends, these principles become a bond for the friendship. A friendship can become a life companion and sometimes a marriage proposal is the result. Love may have some turbulence, so this chapter looks at handling disputes after assessing the agreement to love.

Courtship

Romance can be rather daunting for many people. To rapture love, you find someone and gradually adulation seeps into your life. The idea of love at first sight may be a myth, because a life-long relationship requires a concerted amount of effort, as you will be constantly bringing new ideas to life. Love faces perplexing decisions and there is likely to be apprehension in crossing the chasm from "independence" to "interdependence." Courtship is a time to get to know another person. It explores the possibility of mutual attraction and expects compatibility, even when a wobbling uncertainty exists. Let's cover a new approach to courtship called "the six-month agreement." This agreement has two conditions: 1) To be monogamous, and 2) To not have conversations that imply a long-term relationship for the first six months.

Monogamy ensures you are the focus for attention, and this confirms if your potential partner is prone to jealously or if he or she is faithful and loyal. The second condition is bar none more challenging. This defers a conversation that tempts you to say things about a destiny beyond a six-month term. You agree to not make long-term expectations during the first six months. This avoids the mistake of making a preemptive assumption, due to the intoxicating aspect of falling in love and this gives you an unconventional agreement that bears no conversation about a firm decision until the six-month anniversary date. Both persons have enough time to make an educated choice about dating beyond six-months on this anniversary date. Your courtship might include long-term goal setting and joint financial planning, but this test-drive, or six-month agreement, does not assume a life-term commitment. To make a lasting relationship beyond six-months, when you have enough data to make a decision, you'll feel genuine about the relationship and if this potential mate supports you and perks-up your day. If so, you probably have a good mate. If you feel bored, lonely or you deliberately avoid certain conversations, then you might be leery of renewing another six-month agreement or dating beyond this timeframe. You'll probably need to accept some personality quirks to love someone, but the following statements confirms this decision:

We go to interesting places (beyond dinner or a movie).

I feel this person is attractive (and vice versa).

I feel validated and desirable.

I look forward to spending time with him/her.

We like similar activities.

I am open to his or her suggestions.

He/she has helpful recommendations.

This person has a supportive role in my life.

We have mutual goals.

He/she is willing to help me.

This person is polite and considerate.

We plan events together and call each other routinely.

I feel a special tingle when we hold hands.

He/she shares my fundamental beliefs and values.

This person has invited me to family events.

I avoid some conversations because it will upset him/her.

I think he/she is too adventurous or too boring.

Your goal is to find a mutual set of interests and physical attraction. You look for vital components from the list above. These statements validate your hunches. You can breakaway without hurt feelings, as the agreement implies and ordinarily t is very difficult to break-up at any point. The six-month agreement gives you a safe way out. The liberty to not fear the consequence of continuance or separation is satisfying. There a sense of dooms-day fate on this six-month anniversary date, but a long-term commitment is a vital decision. Let's define this elusive thing called love.

Define Love

Love is a genuine concern for each other. It has an intuitive sense for the other person's needs. Love is not wholly heartedly dependent on one person; it is a shared responsibility. Love is fortified with sensational adventures and bonded to whatever length of time both persons want. Love may be a mutual alliance for friendship or a contractual marriage unity. This alliance guarantees each person's devotion for integrity and quality time together. You share your deepest desires and innermost secrets with this loyal friend, expecting confidentiality in return. You never fear rejection or abandonment with love. You do you make threats or have indiscretions that create problems for someone else. Love provides hope, joy, and open communication. Love includes daily acts of compassion and affection. Love provides a sense of duty, stability and comfort.

We've been told that male and female genders are drastically different in how we love. I question this theory. Gender differences are more related to how we make decisions. Both genders need emotional support. We appreciate sensual attention. We thrive on acknowledgement. We differ in our unique sense of passion and driven ambitions. Men may have a greater need to be intellectually acknowledged, and females may want emotional needs met, but both rely on love as assuring and fulfilling. There may be differences in how we tackle problems. Love consummates how each person handles relationship difficulties and commitments.

Marriage Difficulties

Marriage counseling is very effective at ironing out spoiled, arrogant or selfish actions. Obsessive behaviors like watching too much television, video gaming or gambling are problems that definitely need the assistance of a counselor. Problems can relate to assumptions and expectations. Below are several myths that can bluff even the most experienced lover who thought love was unconditional:

Expectation that a partner should...	Truth is, the partner...
Communicate openly and willingly	Clams up if judgments are made or they fear being chastised
Be attracted to their mate regardless	Wants looks to be impressive
Share financial responsibilities	Must be fair, charitable or just
Explore common interests	Needs some independence
Be naturally inclined to help with chores	Needs to know what to do
Be confident in the relationship	Learns confidence over time

Grumbling at the kitchen sink can be a sign of unmet expectations. It could be a case where one hopes for changed behavior. Couples might be tempted to set up a "give and take exchange" or "I'll do this, if you do that" scenario. This form of negotiation is borderline manipulation. Tactics used to prove love will erode a relationship. Facing one-time problems (such the loss of a job) can be stressful, but reoccurring problems are the root of marriage counseling efforts. You might be apprehensive to say to things that are a nagging discontent. The following statements may help you broach a conversation that addresses concerns related to emotional distancing:

I've realized that I need...

I have lied about...

What I want to do that I'm not doing now is...

I wish we could...

I would like to have this understanding...

What causes love to end? What are irreconcilable differences? Why does a person fall out of love? How did your parents demonstrate love? Have you learned to disagree at times? Has infidelity interfered with a love you've had? It is highly probable that divorce has impacted your life. Of course, an unhealthy relationship can be exhausting for a number of reasons. It could be you had a shotgun marriage proposal that turned into an explosive relationship. Divorce may be the consequence of a teenage pregnancy that prompted a rude awakening in the middle of the night. Most divorces interrupt a family nucleus. We will take a moment to assess how divorce has impacted your life. This is our next exercise.

Δ Exercise 7: Divorce Story (page 128)

Susan Page is the author of *If We're So In Love, Why Aren't We Happy?* She explains how couples are able to establish new behavioral patterns to rekindle a spiritual nucleus in troubling relationships. This may come from embracing a set of principles based on child rearing philosophies. Susan's book has experiments to form a mutual alliance that looks at destructive behavioral patterns. Here we find that couples making agreements to treat each other better. Marriage is complex. There is physical attraction, intellectual needs, emotional attachments and sexual appeal. We will explore sex briefly, and then proceed with conflict resolution techniques that may be applicable for all relationships.

Sex

Sex is a spark that gets the fire going. Love is a flame that needs this spark to continue the burning desire. Romance ignites restraint while at the same emotional desire to feel irresistible. Safe sex may include a condom to protect exposure from a STD, but there is awkwardness in knowing when it is the right time to have sexual urges. Sex may be egocentrically driven. It might be pressured upon someone. Sex might be influenced from the propaganda on television airwaves, which makes it seem so casual. Sex can relieve tension and there is a physically pleasure, but truly this is a complex aspect of our deeply rooted convictions and belief system. Steamy novels do an excellent job at describing the glory of lovemaking—how the erotic pleasure is mystically able to mentally flush all other concerns. That's mighty powerful. In breathless excitement, the memory of sex can linger in your heart for days. Ironically sex is complicated with thoughts of urgency, infrequency, impulsivity and self-indulgence.

Sex is unappealing for some people. There could be medical reasons such as a lack of libido, a numbness of nerves, a lack of internal lubrication, hormonal changes or kidney failure making sex unappealing. There could be emotional wounds that need to heal. Quite often abstinence is a remedy to overcome sexual doubt. Sex can be emotionally satisfying, if you feel love for the other person. Sex requires a spiritual connection in order for it to be meaningful.

Massage stimulates emotional needs with tender strokes of appreciation. A nurturing massage is an excellent way to show love, especially if there isn't an ulterior motive for sex. Massage offers sensory responses from fingertip nerve endings that are as sensitive as lips. A massage can cure an ache, restore vigor and nurture emotional needs. College gives us a chance to explore massage and sex education under one roof. When I attended such courses, it was fascinating to learn "sexual normalcy." I discovered that I must feel love in order to give love. I also realized that there is a natural fear of performance from many people. The notion that sex is a duty must adhere to a loyalty. Copulation to fulfill a lustful desire can be a case of playing with fire. This might lead to futile arguments or an ill matched relationship, so let's learn how to handle disputes before we end this lovely chapter.

Conflict Resolution

Arguments can lead to hurt feelings. There may be times when you need to say, "I'm sorry," but what does this do? It explains your side of a situation, while expressing regret about how this may have affected another person. An apology states, "This is what happened (my action), this is what I can do to prevent it from resurfacing (assurance that my action doesn't reoccur), and why I have regret (the affect it had on you or the other person)." If an apology is due, you shouldn't force this from another person. That's like taking a placebo tablet to stop a heart attack.

Over the past twenty years I have taken many classes related to mediation training. This provided me with the following guidelines for conflict resolution:

- Find the right time and place for confrontations.

- Use active listening techniques.

- Trust that everyone is honest.

- Let people vent their feelings appropriately.

- Set guidelines of what is and is not acceptable in expressing one's feelings.

- Show appreciation that everyone is willing to confront the problem.

- Explain the process involved in reaching a resolution.

- Don't expect a definite outcome from mediation.

- Respect another person's values, because it is likely to be different from your own.

- Deflect aggression.

Active listening implies that one does not interrupt the person speaking. This rule is explained before a mediation session begins. The mediator will explain that the same situation can be described from a different perspective; therefore she will assume that each person has a fair opportunity to speak the truth. Active listening includes relaying what you've heard, for clarification purposes as such, "I think you said... Is that correct?" This avoids anger, because it is an interpretation rather than restating "you said..." which is like putting words in someone's mouth.

There might be two possible outcomes from an argument: to forgive or to agree to not dwell on the problem. The mediator's job will summarize what was discussed and if both parties are inclined to reach a mutual agreement.

Forgiving is the act of confession. Forgiving acknowledges hurt feelings. An apology for a foolish act or how the other person's feelings are respected will open the gateway to forgive. One can forgive, even if an event wasn't entirely your fault. Fault is often irrelevant. To get peace of mind, one must be honest with their role in a hurtful situation. For many, forgiving includes religious intervention such as prayer or confession. If you feel God is ultimately responsible in the act of forgiving, there is still the human responsibility to share the news with people who are impacted with the act.

Forgetting means that you do not fear the consequence of missed information. It requires both persons to agree to forget. Forgetting isn't humanly possible, but reminding a person of their failure is possible. This requires confidentiality. If you agree to forget, there are no recollections, reminders or dwelling on thoughts of the past situation. You are ready to release ownership and not let someone feel regret or remorse because there appears to be no other solution. There should be a mutual agreement to forget so problems aren't tucked under a rug to resurface later.

Aggression can erupt when people expect a specific outcome and they are unable to handle conflict. If you feel you are not handled fairly, anger is a natural consequence. It can be detrimental to reach a conclusion from a single conversation or mediation session, which is formal meeting so both persons explore options. There are three choices to settle a conflict: a win/win, a win/lose or a lose/lose. Legal litigation is most likely to be an expensive battle with a win/lose or a lose/lose outcome (well, this may depend on if the lawyer gets paid quickly). A mediator seeks a win/win outcome, but this is entirely dependent on the parties involved. Mediators stop a meeting if someone is red in the face, their heart is pounding fast or their fist is clenched, because anger is unacceptable. Anger can jeopardize personal safety and it is needless in most cases. Anger should point to a legitimate concern that your human rights were violated. Take two valuable seconds to **STOP** anger. Say each letter slowly when you feel anger—S T O P. This response gives you an opportunity to breathe and let anger calm down. Anger is a symptom of immaturity or a threat. You may notice that anger has a tendency to flee, fight or freeze. Here are the thoughts to consider when you STOP.

S.T.O.P. Anger

S - Sit Down "Is this a vital issue affecting an injustice?"

T - Time "Does this issue need to be discussed now?"

O - Open Mind "What's going on for the other person?"

P - Perspective "Why do I feel anger?"

S will remind you to shut up. T is to access if you are in the right time or place for a dispute. O is to open your mind about the other person's perspective. P will determine if this topic relates to your human rights. The next exercise evaluates how you deal with anger.

Δ Exercise 8: Anger Survey (page 129)

The ramification of making a mountain out of a molehill is relationship deterioration. Maturity is rated by our ability to control behavior. Anger should not be over an issue like having a wrinkled shirt. If you feel anger, when a minor inconvenience occurs, a helpful thought is "Respond, Don't React." This cool slogan came from someone who was particularly calm in just about every situation. A bad relationship has anger; a good relationship does not. Confrontations are important, but only if both persons are cool and collected. Tremendous emotional support comes from love. The bold choice to love with a life long devotion will honor and respect through sickness and wealth. We have a survey that addresses your feelings about finding a mate, keeping romance alive and evaluating foreseeable disputes and this is the final assessment for this chapter.

Δ Exercise 9: Love Survey (page 130)

Honey, I'm home.

Chapter Three: Mindful Fundamentals

Focus on YOU, Baby.

"People are always blaming circumstances for what they are. I don't believe in circumstances. The people who get ahead in this world are the people who get up and look for the circumstances they want, and if they can't find them, they make them."

~*George Bernard Shaw*

Have you ever been fired from a job? Had a major medical trauma? Faced unjust accusations? Had adversity with friends? Exhausted the supply of money while away from home? Been homeless? The game of life can throw a curve ball, even if the best circumstances are present. For example, you could be attending an ivy-league college, but while cramming for exams you have reached mental exhaustion. This chapter explores emotional strife and stress. It looks at tackling stress so wrestling with life circumstances will use mood-altering techniques called mindful fundamentals. This helps you to catch that fast-pitched swerve heading in your direction.

A support network is a group of people who appreciate and support a common good. Strangers can guard confidentiality and give you the benefit of doubt to speak candidly about mistakes. Confession is a crucial way to release bottled up stress. A confession promotes the possibility to restore a healthy self image. Alcohol Anonymous, Shoplifters Anonymous and weight management programs are examples of support groups that restructure life habits. There are many congregations where compassion human beings connect to a social infrastructure so there is a spiritual sense of social belonging. Social acceptance may come from attending meetings or joining a club. This is one example of a mindful fundamental to resolve emotional discontent.

Studies show that children laugh one hundred times more than adults. Kids are allowed to express themselves freely, jump in mud puddles and sing songs without fear of judgment. With an inquisitive and gleeful nature, the concept of personal flaws or blame might be absent. Laughter is good medicine. It brings a chemical reaction to liven our spirit, even when superficially engaged. I heard of support groups in India called "laughter meetings." They literally laugh out loud, and this laugh much different from a mild chuckle as you read an email. Laughter meetings are held in a concrete jungle where oxen, bikes and rickshaw coaches are intermixed in a traffic maze with no clear right-of-way unless a horn is used. A billion people in one mid-sized country have laughter meetings to contrive a mindful fundamental so they can handle stress better.

I developed a program called **Weekly Intentions**. This enables mindful fundamentals as a daily practice in a weekly layout. This worksheet acknowledges mentors, it tracks new habits and it creates a focus for roles and goals.

Weekly Intentions®

Weekly Intentions was designed to clinch confidence. I started this experiment with round river rocks. I wrote the names of all the people I wanted to contact this month. My goal was to be sure I got in touch with distant family members and friends more frequently. Additionally, I wrote words representing weekly goals to visualize an entire set of personal intentions for each month. With thirty+ river rocks sitting in front of me, I realized that my life had a richness I hadn't realized before. I offer value to many people who see me at least once a month. I saw things I wanted to do on a daily, weekly or monthly basis with these rocks. I had rocks for activities like working out at the health club, making sure I reached sales targets on the job, conducting a garden task, playing guitar or saving money. Monthly goals were written on rocks to offer a visual representation of important accomplishments. If I contacted an important person or completed a valuable goal, I moved a rock from a plastic bowl and inserted it to a decorative glass jar. At the end of the month, I gave myself a reward for getting all rocks moved into the glass jar. The reward was usually a sentimental gift with little cost. This experiment allowed me to see that I was intentionally able to focus on valuable relationships and goals most every day. This mindful fundamental created personal pride. I authenticated my key roles and goals in a very appealingly manner.

Weekly Intentions is a worksheet to record this experiment I had with rocks. This improved the flow of managing life intentions, because I see how many miles I walked for example. Five "*I want*" questions align roles and goals with daily activities. In addition, a habit-busting scorecard and a mentor tracking profile were added to this worksheet, after I worked with several life coaches to see how to make life more transformative. As daily interactions are recorded, it captures meaningful moments in life. This worksheet was a snapshot of a weekly journal like no other. I could see what makes me feel good. Extraordinary events were occurring in my life, and these events were recorded in an easy manner. That's when I decided to make a **Life Empowerment Makeover**® component for this book.

You'll notice five *I Want* questions and *To-Dos* on this worksheet, which fosters a dedication to important people and extraordinary things. It takes ten minutes to complete the worksheet at the beginning of the week, and ten minutes to accomplish a task each day. **Weekly Intentions** improves relationships (roles), it acknowledges mentors (brainstorming ideas) and establishes discipline (goals). Follow the instructions below to see how this worksheet is completed.

Δ Exercise 10: Weekly Intentions® (page 131)

I want to be especially nice to _____ this week. This intention acknowledges a birthday, an important person to contact, a networking call to make, or a person who needs companionship. Getting together with this person is optional, but you'll make it definite by jotting down the name of someone you haven't contacted in a long time. It could be you want to do something nice for your boss, co-worker or teacher. Write down a person's name and the *To-Do,* such as getting a mailing address, making a telephone call or sharing a compliment to this person.

I want to learn about ___ this week. This explores something to research or investigate. A learning intention can be to read, to be artistic, to play a game, to study vocabulary words or go to a foreign movie. Learning intentions pinpoints a knowledge-seeking quest.

I want to be engaged in ___ (social activity) this week. This selects an activity such as attending a music event, taking a dance class, going to a community meeting, attending a book reading, finding a workshop, going church, etc. New social outlets offer improved self esteem and this intention gets you exposed to other people in your community.

I want to improve my health by doing _____ x # of times this week. Activities such as biking, hiking, golfing, swimming, playing soccer, baseball, wrestling, paintball, skiing, rock climbing or yoga are listed here. These activities should be fitness oriented. These activities get you off the sofa to circulate the flow of energy in your life.

I want to be involved in the world by doing _____ this week. This might include writing a letter to your congressperson, voting, picking-up litter as you stroll through the park, listening to a public radio station or studying an international topic. As you connect with global events, you broaden the scope of your humanitarian senses.

To-Dos have phone numbers, website addresses, gift ideas or tasks related to the intentions above. To-Dos include a check box that is used when you complete a task.

Mentors are people who offer a smile or humorous comment. Mentors can be famous or local. It could be a clerk at the grocery store, a person who plays ball with their son, a stellar person at work or a politician. Mentors are people who touch your life in a positive way. People who make you think, "Gee, that's nice" are mentors to note in this worksheet. Mentor tracking is very powerful. It acknowledges the actions of other people as a role model, and this can bring new ideas to life. The qualities they exhibit are personality traits that appeal to you. This will draw your attention to appealing health habits, ambitious goals and a myriad of other exciting roles you find compelling. Mentor tracking should occur every other day, so you can feel appreciation of people witnessed in your life.

Habit Tracker®

☐	☐	☐	Meals
☐	☐	☐	Snacks
☐	☐	☐	Workouts
☐	☐	☐	☐	☐	☐	☐	☐	Other

Habit Tracker looks for a number of calories consumed, a fitness regimen or a habit to quit (like cigarette smoking or excessive soda pop consumption). **Habit Tracker** records dietary issues, sleep habits, insulin shots, drinking a sufficient amount of water or taking nutritional supplements. It tracks a behavioral habit you want to observe and/or alter. The other category is used for these suggestions or it can be a conscious effort you want to implement (such as noting how often you interrupt someone when they are speaking). You'll track the frequently of your habits to see if there is a need for a mindful fundamental.

Our principles are evident by our deliberate actions, not our procrastinations. **Weekly Intentions** allows you to observe deliberate actions. It develops an interest in learning new things, going to new places and exploring brainstorming ideas or social outlets. If you use this worksheet routinely, it is an empowerment technique that intrigues you. Claim new insights by adopting mentoring traits you admire. Bust out of an old habit that you don't like. Yearly resolutions are now a myth! This worksheet can detoxify past habits and create a fresh slate every week, creating a desire for continuous improvement and grasping the challenge of life. Activities such as volunteering, going to church, attending a sports club, finding a bowling league or being a cub leader might be extraordinary events that are **Weekly Intentions**. This worksheet invokes interesting conversations, as it is a visual reflection of good things in life. It stimulates enthusiasm and conversations.

The Inner Voice

We talk to ourselves about ninety-nine percent of the time. This inner voice is spiritual guidance in conscious and subconscious thought. The inner voice is the source for self-esteem or self-destruction. This voice restores hope, builds confidence and guides gut instincts. My niece told me that her inner voice must sound like her mother, informing her of potential risks as it gives her words of wisdom when she is trying to make a decision. Our inner voice is a conversation that could be shaken from bad past experiences, making it difficult to have self-assurance or faith in others. It could be too difficult to accept criticism from others or too hard to get out of bed in the morning. Your inner voice may encourage, give compliments or make precautions, but it could be overtly sensitive. If tears flow rather easily, or you are over reactive with remorseful feelings, a hypersensitive nature may be present. This means it is difficult to get feedback from others and self doubt is prominent. Hypersensitivity might prompt a desire to flee, but runaway emotions can be present no matter where you go. A hypersensitive nature originates from a young age to accept discomfort. There could be a fear of confrontation or abandonment. I discovered my hypersensitivity nature was developed when I lived with my Godmother. At the delicate young age of four-years old, a hypersensitive nature intensified over the years as I got bullied into negotiations from my siblings, spouse and parents.

Your belief in self is a reflection of your inner voice. This voice may acknowledge what situations you can alter in your environment. It may speculate success or gloom. We are inclined to think of despair more easily. Mega success may be vague; but disaster is predictable. We train our inner voice to get a strong conviction of potential by attracting positive possibilities, not despair. Training the inner voice should be based on "here and now" powerful mantras that use "I am" comments to reframe and focus on good things. Give your inner voice mantras to affirm personal strengths, confirm integrity and feel empowered. Here are a few mantras that achieve this goal.

I am helpful

I am dedicated to realistic goals

I am improving my health

I am totally loved and desirable

I am open-minded

I am willing to be...

I am no longer affected by…

I am complimenting someone every day

I am able to enjoy social interactions

I am wise and kind

I am trustworthy

I am creative

I am confident

I am helpful

I am fortunate to have active work

Written mantras are ideally posted in places you see daily, such as a refrigerator or bathroom mirror. Stating your mantra routinely, three times in a row, to create a proactive stance for training the inner voice. Mantras are often inspired from music or movies. It can be humorous or even a bit sarcastic, because a joke can spin a positive twist to just about any situation. Needless to say, a chuckle is a mantra in development.

Exercise 11: Write Ten "I AM" Mantras

Be prepared to heal the mind by slithering out of an old skin, like a snake that wears a new perspective after it has outgrown the old self. Self reliance is a skill that comes from training the inner voice to avoid negative self-talk. You have common values with other people and this is often demonstrated with a secret handshake or a verbal nod. Instantly you see similarities with other people and this powerful magnetism provides a place for you in society. Affirmations are accomplishments noted in a journal, but the ugly aspects of life should be listed elsewhere in a DOME Journal.

DOME Journal

Sometimes you will be exposed to chaos or random events that spiral into upsetting scenarios. This is the stuff that puts life in a crisis-reactive mode. DOME journals summarize a negative situation to relieve anxiety. DOME journals include the date, what occurred and educational facts you need to resolve a problem. Here are the components for DOME:

DOME Journal
Date: When did it happen?
Occurrence: What happened?
My Response: What did I do?
Education: What information is missing?

DOME records a legitimate concern, argument or problem. After writing DOME information, you free yourself of mental stress because fret can be constant until it is written. I've actually left an argument, did DOME, and returned ten minutes later with refreshing outlook. I had more empathy for the other person. The next assignment looks at a recent frustration. Write this scenario in the DOME journal provided.

Δ Exercise 12: DOME Journal (page 132)

Ego is self-expression with conscious consideration about your environment and interpersonal skills. **Egotistical** is a self-centered modality where actions or words are focused on self-serving needs. DOME Journals reveal "Ego Type" as Child-Adult-Parent to indicate if you felt stubborn, supportive or competitive during arguments. Here is detailed distinction for these egos.

The **CHILD-EGO** is the playful part of our personality. It has a critical role in wanting to feel love and it has a compelling need to be validated. The child might seek compliments, find humor or be imaginative. It might enjoy spontaneity. It has an enthusiastic instinct to be joyful or blurt out when you are trying new things.

The **PARENT-EGO** has a sense of entitlement and authority. This ego can engage a supervisory role to situations. This ego might say, "I'm always right and I have the final word," because it is your authoritative instinct. This ego is very helpful at nurturing or allocating responsibilities.

The **ADULT-EGO** is an adaptive critical thinker who evaluates risks. This ego creates options and it is inventive with pragmatic options. The adult ego is brave. It declares solutions as if other people should naturally agree.

Egos & Rackets

Egotistical behaviors and rackets are typical reasons for unpleasant circumstances. A racket is a legitimate excuse for a criminal event or wrongdoing that has struck your life. A rack represents the framework for holding on to things. Racketeers are criminals who profit from illegal activities such as bribery or fraud. A racket is a story that holds the framework of actions that create a need to get special treatment. Rackets are hardships that drastically hindered your faith in friends or people. Rackets are scams or acts of betrayal. It is highly possible that rackets create a grudge. When bad things happen to you, it is time for a mantra. Rackets blame circumstances to get pity from others or power to explain a crutch. To relinquish this painful memory, a mindful fundamental will be to track Egos & Rackets. How often you retell a racket or use an egotistical behavior can be observed to develop a life transformation plan.

Empowerment is a discovery process. The first discovery is to look at your habits. You have a choice to accept this behavior or to make a change. Usually it takes six weeks to alter a habit. If you have a tendency to use excuses, blame others, rationalize or justify behaviors, this can have an adverse affect on relationships, health and wealth. The upcoming worksheet is a proactive way to alter bad habits.

Δ Exercise 13: Egos & Rackets (page 133)

My racket occurred after my best friend stole funds that were put in escrow account for a real-estate transaction. She caused me to incur a $100,000 of debt, because her role as a fiduciary broker was violated. She betrayed her profession and the trust of a twenty-year friendship. I had to use mantras to overcome the pain and hurt that comes with when someone's greed has carelessly violated another person. She was a crook and my mantra was stated three times in a row to overcome the pain and to galvanize a new positive outlook. Regrettably, huge losses are very prone to emotional discontent that could lead to depression.

When I learned that about rackets, I noticed how unhealthy it was to tell people that I was a victim of a crime. I was sick of the story and I wanted to regain a level of trust with other people. Repeating the story didn't manifest this likelihood. I decided my mantra was, "I am a loyal and charitable person who will only loan money I can afford to give." I stated this three times every daily for six weeks. A new habit about how I thought about this racket transformed my life. The mantra strengthened my inner voice. It acknowledged that I need not dwell on being a victim. The hardship was compounded with tremendous financial setbacks for the next ten years, but I have good karma. My friend suffered greatly because she had bad karma. At first she stole this money. From here she lost her career, her identity and then the loss of her son. She was incarcerated for other reasons yet she never repaid her debt to me... Needless to say, her actions directly created pain. Sometimes it is necessary to "consider the source" when you have someone who is oozing with bad karma.

Consider the Source

Are some people in your life too harsh, outspoken or controlling? Often these relationships cannot be avoided. It may be a child, spouse, parent, sibling, neighbor, etc. You shield the effect of hurtful comments by filtering out their bad mood, immaturity and rude behavior (the source). Considering the source may answer these questions:

Consider the Source

Will this information make me happier? (What's the **Relevance?**)

Does the source have experience in this matter? (Is there **Expertise?**)

Is there meaningful input here? (Was it important or **Helpful?**)

The source doesn't realize how they cause sorrow. He or she can be a spoiled brat, to which you say to yourself, "That person is who that person is, because that person is who that person is, because that person is who that person is." Replace that person with an actual name. This mantra is helpful when you are attempting to lessen the affect of someone who is belligerent, opinionated or quarrelsome. These attitudes can zap your energy. Sometimes the government is the source. Sometimes a close friend is the source. Your negative self-talk could be the source. Understanding the source will come from the three questions above. When people hurt you, or you hurt yourself, there is a strong likelihood that you might experience some form of depression. When people create emotional pain, it can be helpful to have a mantra that reminds you that yesterday was the past; today is the present, and tomorrow is the outlook that comes from unwrapping your present-day gift.

Understanding Depression

Doctors John H. Greist, M.D. and James W. Jefferson, M.D. wrote a book called *Depression and Its Treatment.* These authors cite statistics referenced by the American Psychiatric Association. They explain that depression can affect people of all ages, creeds, genders and marital statuses. It is an immobilizing illness. Usually the source of depression is heightened by loneliness or a compelling need to reject social conformity. There may be financial difficulties and a grave consequence of suicide. Depression is noticed when there are perpetual sad moods, a loss of appetite, sleep disorders, remorseful feelings and constant fatigue. Depression is a prolonged sadness that hurts. Depression can be triggered by minor mistakes or huge costly errors. It can be environmental or medically explained. Depression can be hereditary. It may be related to a lack of protein and hormone production. Brain chemistry provides a means of calming calm anxiety. One out of five people are likely to suffer from a clinical depression, which could be symptomatic of having difficulty remembering things or having scattered thoughts. If depression symptoms continue for two months or longer, then you should seek counseling.

A book called *Talking to Depression: Simple Ways to Connect When Someone in Your Life Is Depressed,* by Claudia J. Strauss, describes depression. She provides tips to help someone who is suffering from depression. Her book recommends that you not push for communication when someone is depressed. Treat the depression with dignity so there is a focus on rebuilding self esteem. Depression might require routine hugs, biofeedback, acupuncture, pastoral intervention, herbal remedies and physical exercise. As a support person, you might be willing to accept some mood swings, but be sure to set boundaries on what you are willing to tolerate. Depression is curable and you can invigorate the healing process by accepting a supportive role. You might find that multiple forms of therapy at the same time are necessary.

Prescription drugs are common treatment options for depression. This can cease nagging thoughts to some degree but exercise is a very prudent way to produce natural hormones as well. If your thoughts are dominated by perplexing, negative thinking patterns, anti-depressants are effective at stabilizing mood swings or the transmission of cognitive thought. Various side effects such as a dry mouth, sleepiness, spacey feelings and a reduced sex drive are possible. A doctor's assessment must access the use of alcohol and lifestyle habits. A doctor may assess if paranoia (fearing that people are suspicious of you), blackouts (forgetting why you are at a specific place) or other symptoms. Here are some interesting facts about anti-depressant drugs:

> It takes at least two weeks of a consistent medication intake before these drugs become effective.

> There may be hypertension reactions with MAOI drugs if they are taken while your diet has yogurt and cheese. Pickled foods, smoked foods, caffeine, yeast extracts and alcohol will affect these drugs as well.

> Medications will vary based on the cause or diagnosis of depression.

> It is a treatment option that doesn't need to be life-long or addictive.

> People react differently to anti-depressants at various ages.

> Recovery is usually noticed within several months, but some relief maybe noticed within days.

It's best to treat depression sooner rather than later. In some cases you will follow the advice of a doctor, who expects results over a certain period of time. You will rely on mindful fundamentals to reframe your attitude. Doctors should ask in depth questions about your diet and environment, but they may not be aware of mold, dust mites, gas leaks or toxic chemicals in your breathing air. A key means of overcoming depression is to find supportive people that specialize in emotional concerns. The upcoming survey has prudent questions to give you a chance to assess how depression affects your life.

Δ **Exercise 14: Depression Survey** (page 134)

Addictions

Quite often depression is caused by a drug addiction. Our mind processes billions of neurons that branch into various impulsive sensors reactions. This cellular structure is highly prone to addictive tendencies as natural chemical transmitters create reactive responses, regardless if it is a right or wrong decision. You could find drugs cause a chemical imbalance, yet ironically drugs (or alcohol) can be a craving even though it causes misery. Trillions of body cells coordinate brain chemistry, which reaches a final stage of development during late adolescent years. This is when behavioral controlling chemicals fully mature. If street drugs or toxic chemicals are abused, this developmental cycle can be stiffened. This can cause a loss of interest in learning new things. Illicit drugs can influence police citations, facial scars, rotten teeth and dysfunctional relationships. With all these perilous consequences are present, the overwhelming urge to feed an addiction can override logic. Many programs are designed to teach drug prevention, and there is always a need to discuss drug prevention with young adults. My niece wrote a list of questions that I liked, because they were discreet and from a teenager's perspective. Here are her questions:

- What are the long-term side effects of marijuana?

- What happens if I smoke cigarettes?

- How will a drug affect sperm count or a person's sex-drive?

- What have you witnessed with others who have used drugs?

- How do drugs cause a physical addiction?

- What are typical stages of a drug-treatment recovery plan?

- Why are alcohol and prescription drugs addictive?

- What do certain drugs contain, exactly?

- What does a mood-altering drug do to the mind?

- What are the consequences if I were to try drugs?

- How is the brain affected from a drug addiction?

These questions are answered in the book, ***Restore Your Life, a Living Plan for Sober People*** by doctor Anne Geller. This comprehensive guide explains the physiological aspects of drug addictions. She explains how various drugs affect the mind and body. Her book has helped millions of people understand how to seek a life of sobriety. In many cases drug users proclaimed that the addiction started when there was sexual confusion or dysfunctional family dynamics. It is very likely that an addiction can occur instantly from the first time a drug was used. This happens quite often with heroine and meth amphetamines. Some drug dependencies can be related to pain kills and other even household chemicals. Drug addictions can be a long-winded battle with many losers.

Mindful fundamentals are voluntary acts to flush bad memories out of your system to minimize the risk of depression or an addiction. The ego can be deflated when failure is claimed. Mindful techniques affirm good feelings. It might be a mantra, a journal, a plan to handle strife, or a life style that encourages intentional good habits. The older we get, the lonelier life becomes. We've looked for answers to life's most pressing concerns—ranging from self esteem, love and mindful fundamentals—to embrace a better life strategy.

Weekly Intentions is a daily empowerment activity introduced. These tactics are designed to manage the following mindful techniques:

- **Role and Goals** (Circle who you've contacted and the things you intend to do for them in the To-Dos.)

- **"I want" statements** (These are five new intentions for the week.)

- **To-Dos** (These action items relate to new intentions. It might have a detailed description like the telephone number of a person you will contact or a description of something you will do—check the box when your task is done.)

- **Mentors** (Write who inspired you and the appealing personality trait observed.)

- **Habit Tracker®** (Use this to monitor behavioral trends you want to change.)

This chapter is very proactive at assessing how to make a change with habits. In fact it looks at reactive behaviors that are egotistical or based on blaming circumstances. This skill may help you avoid depression, but some discipline is required. Money can be a huge stress. There are many people, including myself, who have had difficulties with money. It can take years to get back on track. Empowerment will be oriented to the supply of money and this brings us to the next chapter, where intentions are financially prepared for the golden years. When you attract positive outcomes, you attract success. If you focus on negative aspects of life, then bad things occur. That's why it is imperative to learn the power of passion so you can attract reasonable prosperity into the life transformation solution.

Life on the Water

On a warm summer day go have some fun

Take a rafting trip in the sweltering sun

If jostled out, point your feet down stream

To deflect the sharp rocks of a treacherous ravine

Target your eyes on a new horizon to claim

Believe in your potential and calm the brain

Float on your back to relax and be still

An embankment will rescue this thrill.

Chapter Four: Financial Empowerment

Find Your Pot of Gold.

"We are prone to judge success by the index of our salaries or the size of our automobile, rather than by the quality of our service and our relationship to humanity."

– Martin Luther King, Jr. (1929-1968)

Is money the root of all evil? Well, let's see... You like money, you need money, and you probably want more money. So, do you play a ukulele to sing another song of hope and glory in exchange for your talent? A hard earned dollar is the result of effort, time, profit and knowledge. Goods are purchased to create the energy of money. This energy ebbs and flows through an economic paradigm of checks and balances. You fondle the energy of money between paper, electronic and plastic transactions most every day. Plastic can be a heavy weight burden in the hip pocket, especially if you sit on a bulge that gets your spine out of alignment. The pursuit of a passion may be unstoppable. This drive can face a conundrum, where there is a limited energy of money but a lot of motivation for invigorating goals. Financial empowerment is a plan to maintain the quality of life, to upkeep social activities and to pursue your dreams. You could be on the brink bankruptcy or on the verge of success. This depends on your feelings about the sufficiency of money. With basic math skills, you can evaluate the energy of money. You will calculate income into percentages and compare these percentages to your spending habits. This is a financial paradigm. It is an ideal budget that knows where money goes. It is a mindset that plans for money to arrive. What happens when you have enough money? How can you resolve not having enough money? Financial empowerment will start when you are free and clear of debt. This will allow you to cross the threshold to financial freedom. Now you can afford the simple pleasures in life.

Here are some interesting facts about money: Over 20 million people in the U.S. are reportedly financially overburdened beyond their means. Half of all bankruptcies claimed today are due to overwhelming medical costs. The national deficit has placed a $20,000 obligation for every newborn baby. One can experience electronic robbery and identity fraud instantly, because it is easy as a click prompting repeat charges even though you didn't realize that a reoccurring fee was contracted. Saying yes on the telephone can transfer a financial risk as well. An excessive use of credit may lead to economic crisis, but there is hope. After all if all hope were lost, what would stand in its place? Money. Let's cover the vernacular for this topic.

Monetary Net Worth

Assets grow in value as time passes. Your paycheck is an asset, because it may increase. Your retirement fund is an asset, because it appreciates until you are old enough to receive a monthly penitence. As skills improve, you become a valued asset, in particular as you continue your education. Collectible automobiles are assets, if they are maintained and protected from hazards.

Equity is net ownership of an asset. For example, a house gains equity when the market value exceeds what you owe on the mortgage. This equity is realized when you sell the home for a profit. Equity is contingent on financing in many cases, of which the charges for interest can be two times the original purchase price.

Liabilities are obligations that require your signature beneath fine print. You've authorized a purchase. This purchase might need insurance for accidental events or a physical disability. Basic necessities, such as food and shelter, are living expenses. Clothing, charitable contributions or tuition fees are different expenses explained in a financial paradigm.

Net worth is determined by calculating equity of assets and all income earned during a lifetime. The energy of money can be retained with investments or items that increase in value. Monetary net worth is determined by listing all income you have earned. Next list assets that you've acquired (minus what you still owe for each asset). Total income is subtracted by the dollar amount estimated from assets to determine monetary net worth. Does it feel like your income has been well spent?

Exercise 15: Monetary Net Worth (complete the above summation)

Taxes obligations, college tuition costs and basic living necessities can evaporate monetary net worth. This may cause you to feel apprehensive about the cost for a college education. This calculation may prompt you to think about increasing your income. A college degree can increase lifetime earnings by a half million dollars. A career can be the most challenging decision to make. To learn more about college and careers, we have a brief summary.

College and Career Insights

When applying for a student loan, you'll find that financial aids are given to most colleges, but this decision is based on number of persons applying and in the student's situation. The financial aid application will ask, "Have you ever been convicted of possessing or selling illegal drugs?" If you have a criminal record, you are likely to not qualify for financial aid. The application fee and an entrance exam are explained at www.collegeboard.com or www.fafsa.ed.gov. Students are required to contribute 35% of their savings for tuition. Parents are asked to supply 5-6% of their savings for their child's tuition. Five million students get financial aid each year. Only half of these students continue to a higher education platform. At a university campus you are bound to find mentors, hear earth-shattering news or be engaged in political events. This inspiration is a wonderful way to live life passionately. Some people are fortunate to have the support from parents for college, but more likely a student will incur the cost.

Back in the day, employers provided opportunities for people to have explorative interviews. This would help potential graduates learn about a specific career or industry. Scheduling an explorative interview has become increasingly difficult to schedule. The website www.lifewithapassion.com (this book name) has an open forum for readers to share experiences about their career experiences. **Career Insights** is the heading used to direct online participants to get gritty details about job descriptions, interesting facts about the work involved and the educational requirements involved. Please share what you liked or disliked about a career into this online blog. Use industry keywords so it is searchable. These unique stories are oriented to a personal description for just about anyone to review. Alternatively, there is a book called the Occupational Handbook. This is published by the Department of Labor. It has formal descriptions about thousands of jobs and careers.

Debt Elimination

It is said that one can get into debt in as much time as it takes to get out of debt. The burden of revolving credit can lead to financial depression. It is possible to pay off debts. This occurs steadily, especially if when there is a focus on a specific debt. With an extra hundred dollars applied to the minimum payment, I was able to free myself from revolving debts in two years. I had a policy to pay 10% of the balance owed or $100 on a debt slated for elimination. In ten months a debt was paid. I have a liberated feeling that the energy of money flows where there are fewer obligations. Financial freedom comes when one avoids debt. Millions of people struggle with financial hardships because they were over zealous with their spending. Excessive debt accumulation can occur. For me there was a sudden loss of income that changed my financial paradigm. I had to make a "hardship request" to creditors during a very difficult year when my life savings was stolen. While I faced financial difficulties, creditors were willing to waive interest charges for several months.

Settlement offers are another option. This is a contract to pay lump sum payments in exchange for a reduced balance owed. This agreement is only considered if the account is in arrears and the debt is subject to collections or legal fees. Twenty percent the balance owed may be taken off the debt, but the makes this decision. Creditors might accept a settlement offer if you prove that you are on the brink of bankruptcy. The offer pays the entire debt in six months. The debt might get paid due to tax returns or the sale of assets. First you'll need to explain how you can afford to pay this creditor, while maintaining other depts. Next you'll need to have a written proposal to explain the amounts you intend to pay and the intervals of each payment. Always get a settlement agreement signed by a supervisor with a fax number and your account number on the proposal. Settlement offers can have an adverse affect on your credit score, especially when the account balance owed was reduced. A "write-off" is noted on your credit report. Creditors are entitled to report the account as a loss. Credit counseling companies and lawyers can assist with written proposals. This may require you to explain why you've encountered financial calamities and you will make the following promises:

- o   I will not incur more debt during my financial recovery plan.

- o   I will focus on one bill at a time and pay minimum amounts for other accounts.

- o   I will close revolving lines of credit after they have been paid in full.

- o   I may elect to keep a few accounts open for credit recovery purposes.

Your next assignment is a financial questionnaire. This evaluates your relationship with money. It looks at yearly concerns, debt prevention, continued educational plans and financial obligations.

Δ Exercise 16: Financial Questionnaire (pages 135-136)

Ideal Spending Paradigm

The Ideal Spending Paradigm is calculated as a percentage of net income— either 40% or 20%. This percentage represents the cost of living necessities, luxuries, social expenditures or investments. Basic necessities such as food, babysitting, health insurance and shelter should be 40% of your net income. Twenty percent of your net take home pay should cover other expenses. A ratio of 40/20/20/20 percentages looks like this:

Ideal Spending Paradigm
Necessity - 40%
Social - 20%
Luxury - 20%
$avings - 20%

Assuming a net income of $2,900 per month (gross earnings of $20 per hour), your Ideal Spending Paradigm looks like this:

Monthly Finances

		% of Income
Net Monthly Income	$2,900	
Necessity	$1,160	40%
Social Expenses	$580	20%
Luxury Purchases	$580	20%
Investments	$580	20%

Necessities are housing costs, food and shelter. Groceries, medical costs and utility bills are included in this total. You may borrow against a social or luxury budget if your living expenses exceed 40% of net income (this is a common dilemma unless you share household costs with another person).

Social expenses cover restaurants, tickets to a show, cell phones, charities, public transportation, tolls, movies, childcare, books, classes, gasoline, beauty/grooming, and personal shopping. Social expenses enable you to leave the house in style.

Luxury items are vacations, cars, boats, loans, clothing, fine art, hobbies, jewelry, life insurance or legal fees. Luxuries enhance self-image, because you are worth it. Living in a nicer community may very well be considered a luxury expense.

Investments are retirement savings, long-term educational plans, rental properties and business ventures. Use 20% of your take home pay for this budget. This allows you to reinvest in your personal skills. It starts with an emergency fund and continues to maximize peace of mind.

Here is an example of a Three-Year Financial Plan where percentages are matched to a gross income of $45,000 a year or net take home of $2,900. This has an increase in earnings and living expenses and an emergency fund that gradually increases over time. Three years is the average length of time required for a financial recovery plan.

Three-Year Projection

3 Year Plan	Monthly	1st Yr	2nd Yr	3rd Yr
Net Income	$2,900	$34,800	$35,500	$36,210
Rent	760	9,120	9,300	9,500
Insurance	190	2,280	2,325	2,370
Food	120	1,440	1,470	1,500
Utilities	90	1,080	1,100	1,120
Social Spending	580	6,960	6,960	6,960
Car Insurance	85	1,020	1,020	1,020
Car Payment	210	2,520	2,520	2,520
Clothing	50	600	600	600
Credit Card	100	1,200	1,200	1,200
Loans	100	1,200	1,200	1,200
Investments	580	6,960	6,960	6,960
Emergency Fund	$35	$420	$845	$1,260

This three-year plan demonstrates how a household budget adheres to the Ideal Financial Paradigm recommended. You'll notice that the amounts indicate that an investment strategy as well as an emergency fund. This fund is an imperative aspect of financial empowerment. When you have funds reserved for emergencies, there is peace of mind.

Emergency Fund

A sudden emergency can lead to outrageous fees, higher insurance costs and incidental bank tolls. If you don't have a fund for unpredictable circumstances, unexpected financial setbacks can compound a bad situation to a worse case scenario. The $2,500 emergency fund demonstrated in this three-year plan could handle an auto repair or some other calamity. This emergency fund should continue to grow. It is said that immediate savings should be three to six times your monthly income. This will make it possible to pursue a dream such as buying a house. There could be a total of $9,000 saved for this fund. What would you be willing to do to get $9,000 now? Would you jump off an airplane to test a new parachute? Would you defer buying a car? Would you quit an expensive habit? A $9,000 gift may give you a temporary sense of financial security, unless you are accustomed to saving this sum of money for emergencies. Lottery winners can end up bankrupt simply because they didn't retain an emergency fund. Ironically scary but true.

Saving $150 a month is the surest way to have $9,000 in five years. If you cannot afford $150 a month, then let's look at a strategy called the tax-yourself fund. This is a fantastic way to track casual spending habits. Stash 10% of every dollar spent into a separate pocket throughout the day. A dime for every dollar is set-aside for the tax-yourself fund. When you are at the grocery store, going to the movies, shopping for clothes, buying a book, eating at a restaurant or filling the gas tank, ten percent goes into a pocket (even if a credit card is used or you have written a check). The tax-yourself fund may exclude mortgage payments, rent or household utilities but everything else is taxed. If you spend ten dollars, you'll need $1 to pay yourself the tax. Put this dollar into a safe drawer each night. In 30 days you might find that $60 was accumulated, which means you've spent $600 on impulse purchases during the month. This tax-yourself technique is a very helpful during a vacation. It reserves some funds for an emergency while you're away from home. The best solution is to plan each paycheck so it adheres to the financial paradigm.

Paycheck Planning

Paycheck planning is an accounting technique to manage future expenses. Simply write the dates and amounts expected from each paycheck interval (or other income sources). Jot your bills and the amount due on the lower portion of this worksheet. When your paycheck arrives, this worksheet has a plan to allocate financial priorities with bills.

Δ Exercise 17: Finance Tracker® Paycheck Planning (page 137)

Finance Tracker is a money journal for paycheck planning and budgets. You might have budgets for investments, children allocations, credit cards, vendors and so forth. It can be an ideal tool for a small business budget plan. It manages an unlimited amount of daily transactions for cash, check or credit/debit activities, with enough pages to span across a year. This booklet may improve your outlook. It has a monthly and quarterly summary as well.

Δ Exercise 18: Monthly Finance Tracker® (page 138)

Your next assignment is to record weekly financial transactions. Notice that your activities can be circled as a Necessity, Social or Luxury cost (N=Necessities, S=Social or L=Luxury). If you were able to invest into a savings account, circle the dollar sign ($). The weekly finance log combines cash, credit and checks into one registry. This is an example of Finance Tracker a booklet solely focused on the concepts of this chapter. Life Tracker is a planner described in the sixth chapter. These two products are designed to support readers on an ongoing basis.

Δ Exercise 19: Weekly Finance Log (page 139)

Investments

Investments are a mixed bag of short-term risk and long-term benefits. You might find it fun to monitor commodities or daily trades for a high-risk yield yet risky "catch me while you can" intrigue. Long-term investing might require patience, as you will wait for a return on your initial contribution in five to ten years. The best investment strategy is a mix of familiar stock ticklers, representing logos you see daily, and innovative short-term investments that might be trendy. At times a Money Market account can be logical place to retain investments, especially if a hard economic regression has occurred. To profit from investments, ask this valuable question, "Is there market demand?" Many people invest in stocks and bonds, because there is little sentimental ownership for that asset. Stock certificates wait for the right time to be sold. I made the mistake of holding onto stock during the high-tech boom and when I needed to liquidate these assets I incurred a loss. I learned that an emergency fund might be best saved in a Money Market account and investment purchases should be made after this reserve has been acquired.

Land, houses, or antiques are investments that might be difficult to sell but they are enjoyable investments to live with. There is personal attachment to these investments, and there accidental risk to these investments. If it isn't easy to sell, it isn't liquid. Ownership can be fun, but be sure you are saving ten percent of your income to a retirement plan. Enjoy life and avoid being a miser who saves too much money, because the energy of money must circulate to gain inertia. Look for liquidity and movement of your investment portfolio.

More often people say that they are too financially constrained to save money, but there are options during difficult times:

➢ Rent a room

➢ Sell goods – (art, jewelry, furniture, cars, etc.)

- ➢   Get a part-time second job using practical skills

- ➢   Make products to sell (cards, pictures, articles, etc)

- ➢   Care for someone in need

- ➢   Establish a new career focus

- ➢   Create a business venture

With this list you can see that purchasing items that enable you to make crafts, focus on career goals and rent rooms in your home can be logical solution to gain additional income. We'll talk about starting a business in the next chapter, so you'll have the necessary information for that option.

Home Purchase

Most people are inclined to purchase a home. This provides a nice tax advantage because there is a tax deduction for the cost of mortgage interest. This is an itemized deduction. This is usually several times more than a simple tax exemption. A simple exemption is calculated as a deduction from payroll. It is based on the number of exemptions you've claimed on a W2. For example, if you earn $40,000 annually, you've probably paid $7,100 in federal taxes (using a standard exemption) from payroll deductions. On April 15th, you claim itemized deductions, such as mortgage interest charges paid, and it is likely to make your taxable income reduced to $22,000. That means you are obligated to pay $2,400 in federal taxes, which means you might get a tax refund of $4,700!

Every twenty years a home needs major repairs such as a new roof, appliances, plumbing repairs, etc. Landscape improvements and gardening could reveal insect problems and other repairs required. You add value to a home with remodeling projects, but this is not a tax deduction until you sell the home. Most people seek increased equity in their home ownership within six years from the purchase date (provided the original mortgage loan is in place). Annual property taxes are usually 1% of your house value or more, depending on where you live. This pays for improved roads, fire, police and schools. You need homeowner's insurance to protect your home from fire, some natural disasters and personal injury lawsuits.

Mortgage lenders assume you can afford 28% of your income for a mortgage payment, property taxes and insurance. Lenders want to see that all expenses are below 36% of your income. Before buying a home, you may need to pay off debts so your "debt-to-income ratio" fits the parameters required for a mortgage loan. Depending on the length of the mortgage term (15, 20 or 30-years), the monthly cost will vary. If you can't pay the mortgage a foreclosure will force you out of the home, unless you have a temporary setback that can be resolved within three to six months. When you first apply for a mortgage loan, "buy-down" points are an option to reduce the interest rate. In 1995, I was able to buy a house with a $6,000 down payment as a first time homebuyer, but that deposit did not apply to buy-down points.

A real estate appraisal can validate if the home is priced appropriately. A physical building inspection looks at structural concerns, such as insect deterioration or previous water damage. Real estate brokers often ask for a commission, which can be as high as 6-7% of the home price. You are able to finance a mortgage with these fees, plus there will be a loan origination fee, underwriting costs, processing fees, title insurance and whatever the lender requires. This can be a surprise when you are ready to sign the final paperwork for a mortgage. When I made a $140,000 home purchase, the amount financed was $170,000—ouch! The property deed is recorded at the county. If you are financing a home purchase, it will be encumbered by the mortgage lien until this loan is paid.

Credit Reports

Companies that gather and sell information about your credit history are called Consumer Reporting Agencies (CRA). Their guidelines fall into the Fair Credit Reporting Act, which is enforced by the Federal Trade Commission (www.FTC.gov) in Washington DC. If you want a credit report or you have a dispute about the information reported, you report this directly to the three Consumer Reporting Agencies:

Equifax (www.equifax.com)
P.O. Box 740241
Atlanta, GA 30374-0241
(800) 685-1111

Experian (www.experian.com)
P.O. Box 2104
Allen, TX 75013
(888) EXPERIAN (888-397-3742)

Trans Union (www.transunion.com)
P.O. Box 1000
Chester, PA 19022
(800) 916-8800.

Any company denying your application for rental, credit, insurance, or employment must indicate what CRA report was used to make this decision. If you have inaccurate information on the report, tell the CRA in writing. CRAs must investigate disputes within 30 days. They will attempt to validate evidence about the dispute, and gather proof that a debt was secured by you. All agencies should be notified if you experience identity fraud. If an item is changed or removed from the report, the CRA cannot put the disputed information back in your file unless a creditor verifies completeness. CRA reports lists inquiries of your credit score within the past two years. Only prospective landlords, employers, creditors or insurance companies have legitimate reasons to seek information from CRAs. A credit report usually contains seven-year data, with these exceptions:

- Information about criminal convictions may be reported on your credit report without a time limitation.

- Bankruptcy information may be reported for 10 years.

- Information reported in response to an application for a job with a salary of more than $75,000 has no time limit on a credit report.

- Information reported because of an application for more than $150,000 credit or life insurance has no time limit for a credit report.

- Information about a lawsuit or an unpaid judgment against you can be reported for seven years or until the statute of limitations runs out, whichever is longer.

www.annualcreditreport.com is a website for credit report information. You will be looking for the magic number called your "Credit Score." This score is based on a complex formula relating to promptness of payments, balances owed, total debts accumulated and credit notations. For example, if you are 30 or 60 days late on a bill, this will appear on the credit report as a line item that adversely affects your total score. To improve your score, you must do two things: 1) pay bills on time and 2) maintain a balance of 50% or less on your total credit limit for each creditor. When your score is over 700, you are usually worthy of a loan, if you are employed. Your next assignment is to request a credit report. You will need to share your name (previous and current), social security number, date of birth and mailing address to one of the CRAs aforementioned.

Exercise 20: Obtain Your Credit Report

Retirement Planning

Tax-deferred investments, such as IRAs and 401K plans are expected to mature until you retire. If you disperse retirement accounts before, there are hefty tax penalties to incur. Retirement plans may be a routine deposit made from paycheck intervals. Some employers match contributions based on a percent you've elected to withdraw. It is up to you to initiate routine deposit funds into a 401K-investment account. These accounts have guidelines, but it is a personal account with elective options for investment strategies. Employers use a third-party fund manager, such as a fidelity organization, to manage the investments. An IRA account is another elective deposit that is tax-deferred until you reach retirement. These elective retirement accounts are restricted to a maximum amount per year ($15,000 or $3,000, for example).

Pension funds are common for union employees. Pension plan are not held in individual accounts. These plans use a calculated contribution that is paid by an employer. There are actuary calculations for the employees enrolled into a pension plan. A third-party financial institution can guarantee the pension trust fund and maintain the investments gathered for a group of employees. There are vesting schedules to project the longevity of funds that will be required when these employees retire. Corporation or government pension funds are usually very secure because there is little chance of dispersing a benefit until an employee has retired.

Retirement planning should include ample health insurance. You might find long-term disability and Social Security (SS) benefits are included in your retirement strategy. You can get a summary of your expected earnings statement from the SS office by calling them at 1-800-772-1213 and asking for form SSA-7004. SS are mandatory for all employees. These contributions go to a national trust, which is only accessible if you become permanently disabled or you have reached a retirement age. SS payments are not guaranteed calculates, but they are based on lifetime earnings. It is possible to earn more SS income than someone else if your income was reportedly higher and subject to SS deductions. Presently the SS trust fund relies on a large percent of working-class citizens. It is one of the largest resource holdings in the world.

Retirees are usually expected to live on a reduced income (one-fourth of a previous employed income in most cases). This income will be a mix of personal retirement accounts, SS and pension benefits. There may be a need to downsize the home and sell stock and bonds, as assets will be used to supplement monthly living expenses. Medical costs may be covered with Medicare, a national health plan for disabled citizens or SS beneficiaries. My father's SS income was $6 over the maximum amount to qualify for Medicare so there is no guarantee of this. Consequently, he had no medical insurance during the golden years. He had surgery performed in Costa Rica because it was impossible to get medical treatment affordably in America. He received professional medical attention and hospice for three months at a fraction of the cost. He learned that financial empowerment requires a focus on health insurance. He retired with a very modest budget.

The Laws of Sufficiency

Calculate 20% or 40% of your income.

Prepare budgets before paychecks arrive.

Be aware of credit use and identity theft.

Only use credit if it enables more income.

Save at least three months of pay for emergencies.

Save at least 10% of your income for long-term retirement.

Chapter Five: Passionate Living

Enrich the Soul. Enjoy the Goal.

Take time to work, it is the price of success.

Take time to think, it is the source of power.

Take time to play, it is the secret of perpetual youth.

Take time to read, it is the foundation of wisdom.

Take time to be friendly, it is the road to happiness.

Take time to dream, it is hitching your wagon to a star.

Take time to love and be loved, it is the privilege of the Gods.

Take time to look around, the day is too short to be selfish.

Take time to laugh, it is the music of the soul.

　　　　~ An Old Irish Prayer

You have a powerful ability to make dreams come alive. A dream can be a harebrain whimsical thought that transforms into intellectual property—an invention or a talent. Dreams manifest with careful planning. I was surprised when my passion emerged, but I had a plan once that dream was clearly defined. Dreams required a fair amount of time, tools and money. It's inconclusive if my dream can survive the harsh reality, but I'll explain the process nonetheless. Here's the origin of this dream:

After several crossroad events—the loss of my father's life, a stolen retirement fund, job layoffs and the loss of my brother's life—I was ready for a life transformation. I dared myself take time off to research my personal credo. I studied the phenomena of passion. I attended training programs and I poured over three hundreds of books to understand personal challenges. Becoming a published author was not anticipated, however it was a whimsical thought ten years ago. I was on an airplane traveling between Africa and Asia.

The value of honoring values struck me years later as I promoted a leadership curriculum for teens. I wanted my life to extend a value to my community that covered a better extent to the program I was promoting. I've incorporated the mission of my parents, my immigrant roots and wonderful life stories to develop a life empowerment program. Budgets had to be established and caution needed to be exercised. I needed to question if I had a false sanguine about this dream. Was this book ready for public exposure? I hired editors, critics and designers to scrutinize the content. Patiently, I waited for others to contribute. This was usually accompanied with an invoice. Personal sacrifices were made as I invested a great amount of time to create this information. Several career opportunities were bypassed and I had a harsh reality to face with consumer demand. Dreams may be difficult to forecast, but the process can be enjoyable.

A long-term plan was subject to timeless content and valuable information in a highly competitive market. This was a tremendous feat. I had to reinvent my forty years of life to make this dream a reality. The idea of wishing for success must have a plan to realize the potential.

Attaining Success

A meaningful mission ought to be encouraged by others, but this is hard to expect. Encouragement may come from strangers, friends or family, yet these sources may be too close for comfort unless they have experience. If you are humble, you might get feedback. If you are unstoppable, you might find it harder to accept suggestions made by others. A riveting sense of clarity comes when you seek improvement. Passion needs rigorous input from others. Your unstoppable drive may be on the road less traveled. You could be easily derailed by apprehension and feel vulnerable as you prove that your idea has merit. Family and friends are particularly good at expressing fear, as they might feel you will be a financial drain or you are facing unnecessary risk. When you are particularly good at letting others be who they are, then they might be willing to help with you. A calling in life is often faced with some degree of doubt.

Are you planning to give up a stable job? Do you feel like leaving the location to which you live? These are hard-pressed options may be related to success attainment. Attracting success occurs when you believe in your potential. Are you convinced that a virtue will be realized with your dream? A talent can be developed with practice, but this requires a dedication of time. A mission statement provides soulful intent, if you know why success will be important to you. Goals can enrich the soul. If the soul is spiritually engaged with virtues, you can guide a journey with inspiration. The law of attraction is a virtue-oriented philosophy. If your calling in life is non-materialistic, there is a good chance your product or talent will be ambitiously focused on helping others (being supportive), empowering your life (loyal to self) or being compassionate (integrity-oriented). These are virtues that are realized when you attain success. Everything you wish for can be a reality, provide the wish is oriented to a virtue.

Long-Term Goals

Goals are terrific challenges. You face financial concerns, hoops to jump through and the need to get assistance from others. As you leap forward in a certain direction, it could feel that you have taken two steps back. Passion can occur at a random moment's notice or it can take years to develop. Usually goals continue well into the golden years. What do you think when I say the word retire? Are you thinking age fifty-five or seventy-five? Do you foresee a trailer or a sailboat? Now we are starting to put PARTS into a long-term goal. Those PARTS are missing details about how, whom and why. Typically a sailor travels to coastal ports with someone who is fearless and able to face survival situations. Hence the mission for your retirement might be, "Before turning sixty, I want to courageously sail the world with a friend. I'm saving $15,000 a year to purchase a boat or be member of a yacht crew." A mission statement describes the Purpose, Action, Resources, Timelines and Special rewards. The special reward is a virtue such as being adventurous or worldly.

It is difficult to explain why goals are risk oriented, but even a harmless pursuit like writing a book has inherent risk. I wanted to spread vibrancy into the world, but that required thousands of dollars and three years time. I was living victoriously, which can be met with resistance. I worked zealously to create this content, but ultimately I had doubt. I saw friends interacting with this content and a splendid thing occurred—they were using this content to transform their life. I made a long-term goal by creating a viable business plan to prove marketability with a prototype. I got feedback to improve the content. The pursuit of passion was exposed to doubt, which is legitimate because it enabled me to improve the content until my emotional turmoil ceased to exist. Several considerations were made to combat doubt, and those seemed to relate perfectly with my professional background.

Signals of Doubt

"Signs, signs, everywhere are signs. Clogging up the scenery and blocking my mind." These words are from a song of my youth. Although I'm from a generation that resisted conformity, the baby boomers have done a great job at erecting signs that usually say, "You ought to..." A life transformation comes when you ought to overcome obstacles that challenge you. This may be to tone down the brilliance of your personal appearance or to avoid the woeful need for pity. It could be blind sightedness of not getting feedback or evaluating the risk of potential failure. There is relevance for doubt—its how our gut instincts operate. It might be your invention needs time to breathe or you need expertise. When an odd feeling occurs as you are doing things you don't ordinarily do, that's to be expected. Here are the steps to keep passion focused:

- ➤ **Make a Mission Statement with PARTS** (Purpose, Action Items, Resources, Timeline and Special Rewards.)

- ➤ **Get Feedback** (Learn what you don't know.)

- ➤ **Identify Fears** (Assess the risks involved.)

- ➤ **Find Distinction** (Unique aspects of your invention or service.)

- ➤ **Develop a Support Network** (These people encourage your skills.)

- ➤ **Collaborate** (These people are hired to expand your talent.)

- ➤ **Build a Marketing Plan** (Be strategic, responsive and customer-oriented)

Wealth comes from making a profit. This may be from someone else's labor or from acquiring things that increase in value. My first business was slated for a three-year lifespan. This is a good example of earning residual income, where time is not dependent on earning potential. It's quite a fun story to share:

In 1989, I was playing a video game and the redundant effort to finish level five was infuriating, so I called the game manufacturer to get a clue. I waited 45 minutes on the phone for the customer service person to answer the call. I got the hint and moments later I was stuck on level six. This was when I realized that there was business opportunity! I purchased several books and magazines for popular video games. A good friend of mine and I recorded video game hints. We used an old computer to build a prototype of 100 voice mailboxes loaded with recordings for the most popular game hints. From here we needed a telephony service company to support a sudden surge of many telephone calls. Engineers at this time hadn't considered the ten buttons on a telephone as a means to spell words, so we had to prove this capability with our prototype.

We hired an animator and live actors to film a TV commercial that used live video dubbed with cell animation. After advertising was aired across the United States, we looked at call reports to determine the best places and times to advertise. Cable television advertising was fairly affordable at this time, so we were able to run spots in ninety locations. We found consumers were willing to pay $1.69 per minute to get their favorite video game hint on demand! I was twenty-five years old and I was an entrepreneur who no longer played video games. I was definitely aware that an increased supply of magazines eventually would become a mainstream option. In fact gaming magazines were sent free of charge to our consumers only three years later. When it was time to close the operation, a valuable learning experience was gained from this venture. We were not on a wealth-driven mission, and that's important. Our mission was to provide accurate information in two minutes or less. We had a fast-forward feature get to a specific game level so it was quick, efficient and easy to use. Our advertisement stated that kids must get parental permission; however we thought it would be best to orient the system so an average consumer would only spend $3.39 per call.

A direct response advertising campaign gave us an easy means of making adjustments as to where and when to air a commercial. A call report helped us plan the cost per lead. When consumer responses decreased, the business stopped advertising. We could have migrated to publishing a magazine or an Internet solution could be crafted ten years later, but our core competency was audio-text and we didn't want to raise capital to start another business operation.

The rock hits a hard surface when you plunge into a financial investment to launch a career or business venture. A product life cycle may be affected by technology improvements and trendy shifts. If your product has a limited life cycle, that's an important assessment to make. You might resolve this dilemma with product updates, new equipment or continued education. Your passionate venture may have an event that changes consumer habits, which was the case with our 1-900-HOT-HINTS business.

Mission Statement

A mission statement should explain your core competency, your breakeven point and the life cycle expected for a goal. Mission statements reveal the virtue you hope to realize. A résumé might indicate your career objective. It explains how past experiences are a good fit for the industry and company you've chosen. You attract a desirable career, based on the virtues you hope to realize with this objective. This establishes purpose with your mission. The next step is to take action. You'll apply for jobs that are in this industry and follow-up with those applications within a given timeframe. There are measurable aspects to the mission statement, such as how much income you anticipate or the location you feel that best suits your career. You'll notice the upcoming example has a forecast of costs and resources that pertain to creating intellectual property. It also has a special reward that stems from a virtue that can be realized from a dream. That's because a mission statement has PARTS – Purpose, Action Items, Resources, Timelines and Special rewards. We will look at the mission for this book and the marketing plans that coincide with this venture. This will clarify the steps taken to pursue a calling in life.

PART$ to a Mi$$ion $tatement

P-Purpose: Create a book on "how to make life transformative" for folks from all walks of life, with timeless recommendations.

A-Action: To study and write for three years, developing a series of tools that support readers with ongoing solutions.

R-Resources: $4,000 is needed to print the first 200 copies of this book, which includes the cost for editing, graphic design and website creation. $16,000 is needed to print and distribute 10,000 copies. A breakeven point will occur when 2,000 books are sold.

T-Timeline: To have mainstream distribution in place within six months of the finished edition of 500 books in print.

$-Special Rewards: To get testimonial letters from readers stating how this book affected him or her. To improve a writing talent.

Critical decisions were evaluated from this mission statement. It was clear that in addition to dedicating time, I would need cash. With the help of a Pro/Con list, I was able to access if spending $4,000 or $16,000 was worth the risk.

Pros & Cons

Benjamin Franklin used a piece of paper with two columns to make important decisions. One column simply stated "Pros" for benefits he hoped to achieve, while the other column indicated "Cons" for the risks involved. Benjamin assessed how benefits outweighed disadvantages. Every long-term goal was put into motion with this analysis.

I add two multipliers to my Pro/Con lists. 1-3 is a multiplier based on my how much this benefit or drawback means to me. For example, how important is it for me to improve my writing skills. Well on a scale of one to three, it's a crucial skill, so I ranked it as a three. The second multiplier is 0-5. This ranks the significance of this benefit overall to the risk and benefit. How significant will this decision influence the benefit of improving my writing skills. Next, I do the math and multiply "Personal Value" to "Significance" to reach a conclusion of my decision. Here is an example of that analysis:

Pros

+ Personal Value Multiplier	Significance	Score	Total
3-Improves my writing skills	+5	15	15
2-Enables a public speaking career	+5	10	25
1-Provides expertise	+4	4	29
2-Becomes a legacy for grandchildren	+2	4	33
3-Uses my background in marketing	+4	12	45
3-Engages me in things I love to do	+5	15	60

Cons

-Personal Drawback Multiplier	Significance	Score	Total
3-Costly venture	-5	-15	-15
1-Personal letdown	-4	-4	-19
2-Writing critics may not like it	-2	-4	-23
3-Failed venture	-3	-9	-32
3-Focus away from other priorities	-4	-12	-44
1-Requires web design skills	-2	-2	-46

Overall Score			+14

A positive outcome was analyzed from the Pro and Con list, but there is still the difficult question of justifying the cost of $4,000 or $16,000 to start this business venture. I needed an initial test market to make this decision. A business plan to determine viability of this goal is the next step.

Business Plan

There are various stages for a business. At first there is the infancy stage, where an idea or prototype is produced. With a beta product one is able to get feedback and test various marketing efforts. From here a business plan will be developed to forecast costs and customers. This will coincide with due diligence, a process to evaluate improvements that are needed. As money is needed to package a product or service, the specific location becomes an integral part of the plan. This plan will look at distribution methods, safety, liabilities, insurance and advertising. All of this is updated as time progresses. After all, a better-made mousetrap will gather dust unless it is promoted. Here are the components of a business plan:

- ✓ **Target Goals for Production & Sales**

- ✓ **Design Prototypes with Optional Features**

- ✓ **Estimate the Life Cycle**

- ✓ **Assess Unique Distinctions** (Compare this with competitors.)

- ✓ **Collaborate with Expertise**

- ✓ **Assess Operational Costs**

- ✓ **Develop Marketing Plans**

You might fantasize about prosperity, but in reality you are wearing many hats and spinning several plates at once when a new business is launched. You are a master of all trades and yet focused on a single objective. To wrap your arms around that key objective, talent might need to be refined. It could be a powerful golf swing, an operatic voice or an ability to guide a raft in the wilderness terrain. As you work on improving talent, you create opportunity—which is a matter of being in the right place, at the right time, with the proper tools to demonstrate knowledge and skill. You control a potential destiny with wisdom and tenacity.

Mundane tasks such as maintaining a website, making calls, updating the press or studying for an exam should be expected. Passion requires endless hours of dedication. You might be suited to hire experts to add efficiencies to your operation. Expert advice looks at your distinct features. Budgets are analyzed and milestones are established based on your product features and specific audience. You'll need to know how your product can benefit consumers. Your solution might be oriented to saving money, adding greater efficiency or bringing personal enjoyment. The only thread of hope in today's business world is that consumers buy products with a perceived value. You'll need a marketing plan to achieve this goal.

Marketing

Where to market is as critical as how to market. To sell goods, you'll advertise with keywords to draw people to your site. Your product may need a language translation, if it is better suited to a different country or audience. The most important aspect of starting a business is location. If your solution is exclusively available in the United States, then your strategy will be to appeal to that local market. Critical decisions are made to create distinction about your goods and services. A brick and mortar business has the company name etched name on a plaque to draw customers to your site. The marketing message will show benefits for a consumer who goes to the site. A customer is usually looking to spend money on things that improves the quality of life.

Marketing incentives offer some degree of impulsivity. It may be a coupon, a free add-on service or an extended warranty offer. Incentives could be oriented to getting a referral in exchange for a price advantage. Customers most likely need a sales person to drive the process to help them make a decision. The most important aspect of salesmanship is integrity. This means a salesperson is attentive to the needs of a customer. A salesperson will ask the critical question of "Wouldn't you agree?" This confirms a buying decision or it will open communication for concerns. Objections are a sign that your consumer needs more information. Integrity selling is an honest representation of your price and long-term benefits. Integrity selling addresses the explicit needs of a customer so get permission to have a decision made. You might need to confirm what is the best time for a consumer to make a purchase decision. An unhappy customer experience will be retold ten times more than a testimonial; therefore it is imperative that customers are impressed with the responsiveness of a sales process.

Advertising is quite different than branding a solution. Most television commercials are oriented to creating a brand image. Many advertisements are oriented to prompt a direct response. Marketing gets to decide if branding or a direct purchase is the objective. Marketing will clarify product differentiators. Marketing develops a strategy to make it easy to order. Marketing sets price expectations based on competitors and value. There are several marketing plans that occur simultaneously. The transparent nature of these activities were outlined in my business plan, which includes the following:

Plan A: Sell to specific industries using several hundred free copies for libraries, bookstores, schools and non-profit organizations to preview the product. (This plan identifies **industries** and prototypes needed for a "try and buy" solution.)

Plan B: Replicate marketing efforts in strategic cities located in the Pacific Northwest. (This represents **geographic areas** to market.)

Plan C: Promote workshops to hospitals, community colleges, drug rehabilitation centers, churches and youth mentoring programs. (This plan looks at **networking opportunities**.)

Plan D: Go beyond search functions at Google, Yahoo or MSN. Find strategic online relationships with organic keyword attributes, making it easy for customers to find the website to place an order. (This plan provides an **online ordering system**.)

<u>Plan E:</u> Expand distribution sources to specialty stores and superstores. Bundle tools together as a gift solution. (This plan broadens market presence for **alternative sales outlets** and a higher **value per sale**.)

<u>Plan F:</u> Advertise on a city bus, on radio and television. Distribute a CD for respondents as a prospective marketing tool. (This plan exposes the public to **brand name recognition** with a free trial incentive that is easy to ship.)

<u>Plan G:</u> Attend tradeshows and public speaking forums. (This plan provides a forum for **due-diligence** and engineering ideas.)

Marketing plans promote products and services in different venues. I've applied these plans for various businesses, including services. There are many decisions that evolve with goals. Pro/Con lists identify risks and benefits. Once a decision is made to launch a business, the mission statement will drive action items, resources and milestones. That's the secret to attaining success—there is a leader who has a universal spirit of strength. This inner strength comes from fully understanding one's virtues. Virtues will enrich the goal to enlighten the soul. As one spends a great deal of time developing a passion, there is a need to continue education and practice success routinely. Passionate living techniques are now available on monthly calendars.

Δ Exercise 21: Passionate Living Month of____ (page 140)

Success is getting what you want.
Happiness is enjoying what you get.

"The real difficulty in changing an enterprise lies not in developing new ideas, but in escaping from all the old ones."

~ John Keyes

Chapter Six: Personal Freedom

Managing Independence.

"We all have to do the best we can. This is our sacred human responsibility."

— *Albert Einstein*

Personal freedom is an ability to demonstrate discipline and imagination. We look at leadership skills, visualization techniques and organizational techniques so pursuing a passion is well defined. There is wisdom, foresight, and liberty that creates the backbone of our social values, yet there is also a civil duty to adhere to the code of conduct.

Leadership

Leadership inspires others with a strategy to attain success. Success is satisfying, especially during moments of tranquility. Success occurs when there is discipline to practice an art so skill is developed. Be it far-reaching as the Olympics, or close to home at a local speech group, you can be a champion. Leadership combines goals with imagination that is oriented to future possibilities. As you develop ambition, the target is like an archery game, you must **AIM**:

> A–Attainable Goals
>
> I–Imaginative Visions
>
> M–Milestones

Let's explore the definition of imagination from *Webster's Collegiate Dictionary*: **Imagination: 1) the ability to visualize or form images and ideas in the mind, especially things you've never seen or experienced directly. 2) Resourcefulness and having the ability to construct solutions to difficult problems. 3) To act creatively with a semblance of reality.** Imagination is able to feel the height of a leap, the distance of a throw or the anticipation of a maneuver. Before the team enters the playing field, momentum is reinforced with **AIM** objectives.

We started the empowerment process with **Weekly Intentions**, where a list of appealing characteristics of role models and mentors are listed. This list may be used with a life coach. My coach started each session with three questions, and my response is in parentheses:

Who are you willing to be so I can be affective? (Am I willing to be attentive, communicative, empowering, flexible and receptive?)

What are you are hoping to achieve? (My goal is ___ with a specific timeline of ____. The mission statement is ____.)

What is the measurable outcome you anticipate? (I will focus on these important tasks _____, which need to be accomplished by _____.)

A coach uses mentoring qualities from **Weekly Intentions** (such as being athletic, artistic, compassionate, courageous, dependable, direct, energetic, honest, helpful, intelligent, loving, loyal, peaceful or worldly). The answer for the first **AIM** question is oriented to traits you admire the most. These questions can free the mind of previous concerns, and it instantly establishes a focus for the coaching session. This can then progress to crafting a vision of success.

Visions of Success

A two-hour daily siesta is a time allotment for families to share lunch together while shops, schools and public services are closed. This is common in European countries were Personal Time Off (PTO) becomes a daily event. PTO is a valuable aspect to life. Saturday is defined as the seventh day of rest. Even sporting regimens have PTO. This time-off can decompress stress, just like an airplane before take-off. Use this time to jog, walk or close your eyes for twenty minutes. You might meditate to extend the mind into an imaginative thought about success. During meditation, you are able to visit an exotic place, buy a ticket to a show or go an enchanted spa. See if subconscious ideas spark potential where there are no limits to your abilities. In just a moment, you will get a guided meditation. Starting from the tip of your toes, imagine stress being lifted out of your body. Breathe in through your nose and exhale stress out of mouth. Let your mind follow the bloodstream. Feel circulation move from your legs, into your pelvis, stomach, heart and arms. You might find a stress point. Does stress occur in your spine, stomach, lungs or eyes? Tension may be linked to an underlining subconscious concern. For example, tension in your stomach may be oriented to absorbing stress or having diet concerns. Find a stress point and create a visual thought about a competitive sport or a banquet of raw foods when you meditate to ease tension. An abstract or opposing thought related to the tension may be helpful. The upcoming *Visions of Success* meditation attempts to guide a vision for ideal relationships and career options. Have a friend read the following passage out loud. Please be in a relaxed place, where you can lay down and let tensions ease. Do not drive a car while listening to this audio program. This meditation should inspire teamwork and long-term goals such as owning a home, remodeling a garden or being creative with kids. Now we are ready to proceed.

Exercise 22: *Visions of Success* Meditation

During a dream state, imagine the attainment of success. Plant ideas for the subconscious mind and think of microscopic images that reveal enchanting passions. When you are fully awake and revitalized jot down the images you saw. For now, close your eyes and relax. Let your mind drift like an ocean float, moving back and forward. Back and forward. Back and forward. Back and forward. Waves are splashing quietly at a distance.

You are in a sacred, peaceful place where the sun heats your body. This radiant energy touches your feet and moves into your legs and upper pelvis. Heat penetrates into your stomach. It spreads through your circulatory system while your mind is at peace. Those squiggly lines on the back of your eyelids are going up and away. Tingling sensations move into your arms and neck. Your spine is relaxed, and your fingertips are completely free of tension. You feel a soothing sensation from the forehead to your eyes, as your body floats in weightless suspension, like an ocean float moving back and forward, back and forward, back and forward. As you fall into a deep slumber, Visions of Success will be formed.

Think of situations in your life when you were really happy. Remember back in the day when it snowed and all the kids in the neighborhood actually played together? You made igloos or sledded down the driveway. Was there a special place where you could hide from others? Remember the enthusiastic joy of jumping right in the middle of a large mud puddle or skipping a pebble across a lake? Let your mind drift into the dimensions of the outer rings. Imagine your feet touching soft sand at the shore of a large body of water. Your entire body is at ease. Your eyes are closed and there is no temptation to open them.

On the horizon there is a fantastic vacation home painted in your favorite colors. What colors do you see? There is a beautiful garden in front. It has lush plants you admire. You are walking up the driveway and there is a mode of transportation you've always wanted. Is this vehicle a motorcycle, a carriage, a bike, a helicopter or a walking stick with wheels? What do you see when you look inside? Your fingers stroke the curves of this sturdy construction and glossy coating that has a texture unlike the cold metal you had before.

At the front of this house, there is a place to clean and dry your feet. A soft rug welcomes your arrival to a foyer with cool tile. Bracing your entrance for a temperature adjustment from the outside to the warm interior, there are decorations and furniture welcoming your arrival. Here you see representations of many places you have traveled. This room is serene as you walk down the hall to the master bedroom. Beautifully framed are the photographs of your life. You find a change of clothes in a closet with intricate carvings hung from the walls.

Someone is approaching. This is your spouse. What does this person look like? You feel the love connection instantly as this person comes into view. In their presence, you realize how your achievement has made this person very content. You smile a peaceful satisfaction that fills your heart completely. On the bedroom door there is a lush robe with your name monogrammed. The robe has a soft, luxurious fabric that you caress. This amazing feeling of gratitude is enhanced as you slip into a comfortable pair of shoes. Everything is orderly as you walk into the adjacent room to turn on the lights. Here is the most spectacular bathroom imaginable, with a fancy brass fixture that reminds you to touch the splendid granite countertop texture below. Your fingers naturally glide across the surface as you grab a soft cloth dry your face. The soap has an aroma that you relish and the linen rack that has pre-heated the towel. You look at the bathtub and realize the view from the window facing your backyard represents hundreds of old growth trees and a grassy field yonder. That's where several horses roam. You think about the riding school attended last year.

Your swimming pool was just cleaned and the backyard is stunning—flowerbeds are landscaped to extend the beauty of your interior decor. Even the tennis court looks perfectly maintained, which is surprising because you permit the community to enjoy this portion of your property. You look out the window a few minutes longer to soak in the wonderful views and a fresh breeze wafts in. This is when you recognize the smell of breakfast.

At the dining table there is a banquet of food igniting your hunger. Your family stands at the table. There is something special you would like to say to everyone this morning. You feel so good, but they already know this. You choose to sit down and say grace instead. What words of thanks are spoken? When breakfast is done, you'll be sure to tell everyone how much you love them. A fresh bouquet of spring flowers was put in the center of the mahogany table. You let your fingers slip through the petals and take a moment to smell the roses. That ignites other sensational feeling for this day.

You will be meeting a press agent to explain success. You express how you got your initial inspiration. You acknowledge coworkers and people who helped you. What will these employees tell the press agent? Who are you thinking of this very moment? Did these people join your business because they were your best friends? The press agent asks how much compensation you received last year? Of course, you won't say, but you think of a number nonetheless. Yes, life has been good. You have helped thousands of people in this world. A *young child, whom you don't know, is blessed by your invention. You look around the office and see next year's design in a chart or drawing. Is it a storyboard, a movie, a report, an advertisement or a certificate? You glance closer to see the details in this document. What does it say?*

You finish work and at home someone is chopping vegetables and making fresh ice cream. What do you say to this person? This person is curious about your day. You taste the food and it melts in your mouth. Now you have no words to say other than ummm. You have the urge to relax in the den for a half hour before dinner. Here you see a hobby in the studio as you walk past. You think about that project for a moment. It beckons your attention. What craft waits inside this room?

Evening has come so you place a silk comforter on your neck and you are anxious for another day. You know how valuable it is to close your eyes. You greet tomorrow by springing out of bed with enthusiasm. Soft laughter floats at a distance from your window. The sound of ocean waves fills the background once again. You take a long sweet moment to clear your mind and feel the power of relaxation grace the spirit inside. You are grateful once again and look forward to spring out of bed tomorrow.

This meditation is primarily focused on prosperity and personal achievement. It is designed to create a liberating sense of leadership. There are tools used by leaders to enable success. These tools are integrated into this book, so we'll take a moment to briefly describe these tools.

Life Tracker®

Success masters teach the skill of time management, which is important if you feel that there isn't enough leisure time. The secret to time management is to schedule tasks such as doing chores, getting exercise or relaxing, because these might be ignored tasks unless one makes a promise to do it.

Every hour increment from 5:00 AM to 12:00 AM is listed in column on the right side of **Life Tracker,** a planner that is printed every six months. This planner has monthly calendars and paycheck planning worksheets, plus it combines time and money management into a unique weekly layout that spans across four pages. Weekly finances can emphasize spending habits from all three sources—cash, checking accounts or credit cards. Every other day you are able to record a mentor and gratitude statement. This planner is conveniently sized to go everywhere you plan to be with a sturdy cover and flexible spine. Best of all, it doesn't require a battery. You can back-up your electronic caller ID list with the swipe of a pen using the contact section provided. This planner is dated in a unique manner as well. This semi-annual solution starts either in January or July.

Δ Exercise 23: Life Tracker® (page 141-143)

Organizational Journal®

Disorganization can be a huge stress and waste of time. Quite often too much clutter is a burden and we simply need to assign a home for things scattered about. There are so many things to remember: passwords, websites, movies previews, vacation sites, etc. All of this information may be tethered to a computer or it is bouncing around in your mind waiting for the right moment to be accessed. It is possible to retain such information in an **Organizational Journal.** This has fifty-two alphabetical pages for random information pertaining to the index below. If you have something to record that is not listed as a topic, simply add a new topic to the index. The journal captures information such as a famous quote and inspirational ideas, because we are all vulnerable of having valuable data lost to a memory bank malfunction. My journal is near the telephone, so I know where it is located when I need to record a spontaneous bit of information I've seen or heard. Here are the index topics for this journal:

A-Z Index

A-Airlines, Automobiles

B-Babysitters, Banks, Birthdays, Books

C-Camp Sites, Credit Cards

D-Dining, Dentist

E-Education, Email

F-Family, Friends

G-Grocery List

H-Hotels, Household

I-Insurance

J-Job History / References

K-Kids

L-Login Names

M-Medical, Movies Previews

N-Neighbors

O-Other

P-Passwords, Pets

Q-Quotes

R-Restaurants

S-Savings

T-Taxes

U-Utilities

V-Vacations

W-Websites

XYZ-Yearly Questions

This journal includes a three-month supply of **Weekly Intentions.** That is ideal for someone who is inspired to conduct a life empowerment experiment. The **Organizational Journal** might be used to record a conversation with a vendor, teacher or doctor. It can record automobile repairs. You might even list a history of tax payments. It captures information that you want to access in the future.

Personal Billboard

Personal billboards are constructed to reflect goals, joyful words and mantras. The billboard is a tool to visually represent your life. My example in the Appendix has words printed from the computer. It is actually a large font that can be read from a distance. To make a billboard more effective, use words clipped out of a newspaper so it looks like a ransom note. Make a declaration using humorous or serious words to describe your interests. If you enjoy skiing, where freedom is mingled with cool air and high jumps off treacherous mountains, find a photograph of this for your billboard. Creating a personal billboard takes a couple hours to complete, especially if you need to buy a few magazines. This billboard is a fun activity and it gives you a chance to search for photographs in sports, travel and lifestyle magazines with intrigue. You'll find photographs visually representing your goals. I have

photographs of people biking, golfing and romancing in the example
provided. There is a picture of wall-to-wall hardwood floors, which is my next
home improvement goal. I clipped fifty pictures before selecting these and I
added a photo of my face to place on the yoga dancer. This shows that I am
doing these activities. I used an acronym for my name. I have another
billboard focused on a thirty-pound weight loss goal. Personal billboards are
a collage of the upcoming three years or an immediate goal. It is your
advertisement for the future.

Δ Exercise 24: Personal Billboard (page 144)

Elevator Speech

An elevator speech is a personal introduction used when you meet someone
at the grocery store, in a job interview or at a restaurant. This speech relays
valuable information where you have four things to express:

- Who you are

- Where you are coming from

- What you are looking for

- How the person you are addressing can help you

The purpose of an elevator speech is to reveal vital information that opens a
conversation. The respondent will reply with this thought:

- Are you honest about your representation?

- Is there a purpose with your introduction?

- Is there a connection between you and me?

- What is the call to action?

The elevator speech is very brief. It contains twenty words or it is expressed in twenty seconds. There are various elevator speeches for different settings. It's important to think about your elevator speech when you create a personal billboard. My elevator speech is this, "I am an author of a life empowerment program that was designed for many age groups. Do you know someone who might be interested getting a copy of this book?"

Exercise 25: Write an Elevator Speech(s)

Personal freedom is leadership. A coach demonstrates leadership in a humble yet effective manner. We all have the responsibility to stand in line at the motor vehicles office so we can get a driver's license renewed. We show up, demonstrate skill and prove our environmental consciousness with a certificate that proclaims if our vehicle is emitting a small amount of carbon pollutants. As I've sat in this office, I wondered if a famous person would glide through the door. Virtually everyone has this responsibility, if they want to have the liberty to own a car. The impact we have on the planet is curtailed as a responsibility. Personal freedom is a license for passion. It is a set of coaching tools to motivate self and others. It gives us driven ambitions that is handled carefully, not carelessly.

A Time Continuum

Focused on things that matter most
Safeguard this sacred ghost
Pass through the millennium
On an infinite time continuum.

Chapter Seven: A Positive Attitude

Be Happy. Don't Worry

"To become self-actualized, we need two things, inner exploration and action. The deeper the self-exploration, the closer one comes to self-actualization."

– Abraham Maslow

A positive attitude is omnipresent. It is a switch that works perfectly most every time you engage the trigger. Unless a flash occurs, you essentially trust a light to function and tools to work. This faith can explain how a positive attitude comes from being a guiding light for others. Our attitude can influence others to use their special gifts. They are as follows:

- To support others

- To build things

- To entertain

- To heal others

- To provide encouragement

- To be creative

- To inspire people

These gifts can improve one's outlook. It is essentially a faith in goodwill for all of humankind.

National Pride

"Anyone can hurt you, if you let them" was a quote from my neighbor. He shared his views on having a positive attitude by saying, Stephen King would say, **"An event is either purposeful, random or chaotic."** Maya Angelo would say, **"If you don't like something, change it. If you can't change it, change your attitude."** President Nixon would say, **"The only way someone who hates you can hurt you, is if you hate them and then destroy yourself."** I liked his quotes, because they come from a perspective I haven't considered before. When I think of Nixon, I realize that he changed the Cold War by enhancing trading power with China. This has changed our global economic viewpoint forever. I felt pride for him while watching the opera, Nixon in China, yet he was my least favorite President.

When I pledge allegiance to the flag, common values are shared with fellow men. This reminds me of a motivation seminar, where Mr. Colin Powell spoke. He is a former US Secretary of State. He said he wanted to see a revolutionary change in how people consume energy and select health care. Mr. Powell shared stories about the experiences he had defending the security of our nation. This has given him great pride, and he is definitely a mentor. We shared common values and this was recognized as he said something to entice laughter to ease the serious nature of his message. Mr. Powell had an important message to share: There is nothing to fear in the playing field of compassion, yet there is tremendous fear that exists in the battlefield of war. Madeleine Albright, also a former US Secretary of State, spoke at World Affairs Council meeting. She shared this message: Terrorism cannot change our values as a nation. When a prevailing injustice is happening somewhere in the world, political parties are there to help threatened societies. Our hope is that diplomacy, economic sanctions and international laws govern common principles, because behind the body of United Nations are compassionate people.

Planetary sustainability is a concern for everyone. We have a responsibility to protect our environment for future generations. This might entail changing some habits towards green-consumerism. "Reuse, don't abuse; recycle whenever possible." That's my mantra. I attempt to decrease the impact I have on this planet with this mindset. This forces me to purchase things based on planetary concerns. For example, I buy eggs packaged in a cardboard box versus a Styrofoam carton. I go to a farmer's market to avoid buying imported products. My propensity to adhere to planetary responsibility includes the following activities:

- Avoid purchasing things that will be discarded soon.

- Call companies who send junk mail and ask to have your name removed from their mailing list.

- Put raw food waste in a yard compost enclosure.

- Pick up litter, when you see it.

- Conserve water, electricity and fuel consumption.

- Campaign for planetary environmental concerns.

➤ Engage kids in outdoor activities.

➤ Vote for policies that ensure fresh air and more public spaces.

➤ Preserve wildlife when possible.

The Roman Empire became a crumbling society after entertaining citizens with bloody violence to execute criminals. This was barbaric and short lived. The coliseum didn't have a reenactment—it was the real deal. This civilization may have destroyed the core essence of human compassion with these brutal acts. Interesting that the strength of this society crumbled to pieces. National pride is vital for everyone. This includes having concern for the welfare of others, therefore a principle everyone is equally important overrides the idea that we are better. Economic wealth is interdependent of wealth nations to extend goodwill, while we strive to maintain a middle class society that has morality.

Sincerity

The word "sincere" comes from Latin roots originally described as "without wax." Ornate decorations made from wax molds were used to create façades on buildings instead of original carvings, which were sincere. Sincerity is evident from words and actions identifying a purpose and attentiveness to one's calling in life. Being bloated with money can throw integrity off balance. I once heard a well-paid athlete say that he wasn't clear what integrity means, so I thought I'd clarify this point.

What is Integrity?

Actions are consistent with your words. *(Honest)*

Roles and goals are well defined. *(Attentive)*

Activities reinforce core values. *(Purposeful)*

Does integrity represent a different set of values on the job versus at home? Did you learn honesty at school or from your social environment? How can you reinforce integrity? These answers come from your inner voice. Your story reflects lessons learned from parents, bosses, teachers and friends. Some people are influenced to lie, based on their environment at home, work, school or government. Gossip is a violation of integrity. Being discreet with information entrusted to you is an act of integrity. One might say "I'm not the source of that information" or "I'm not willing to repeat what someone else said" when confidentiality is questioned. A genuine sense of integrity is the gateway to perpetual happiness.

Be Happy

There is a book called *The Art of Happiness,* by His Holiness the Dalai Lama and Howard C. Cutler, M.D. They compare Asian philosophies with Western ways. Doctor Cutler summarizes how Western continents tend to perceive pain and suffering differently. We account for everything through an analysis or explanation—whether it is brain chemistry, cultural conditioning or cognitive thinking skills. We make a determination to ease suffering by conditioning fear with medicated options to cease the pain. Fear is a human survival instinct that sparks discomfort. This trigger is a mechanism to respond differently the next time a situation occurs.

His Holiness the Dalai Lama has an interesting a set of beliefs that explain how to establish a different outlook on life. Love and kindness opens the door for happiness, especially when you believe humans are just like you. Faith in our society is imperative. Happiness swings with varying degrees of optimism and disappointment based on situations you didn't expect and predicted circumstances. You have power to amplify negative results, especially if you've been programmed to crave or hate. Positive thinking is a belief that most people are fair. You believe that everyone deserves to have good things happen. A positive attitude is benevolent to trauma or suffering to a minor degree. There is an overwhelming hope for the present-day to be a choice, not a rationalization. In order to interrupt happiness, positive thoughts need to be present during even-keel and off-kilter moments.

Even-Keel is a when most everything is perfect. Interpersonal skills are good and you are able to coast along the comfort zone with reasonable prosperity. If you are somewhat satisfied with social outlets, you use empowerment to develop a vision of success, which may come from creating some form of intellectual property.

Off-Kilter moments are traumatic events that spin into a high-anxiety situation. This is when emotions are tempted to runaway. Empowerment is used to actualize a change and face life transformation boldly. You make a declaration to accept challenges, so you can be a stronger person. Triumphantly, a positive attitude relies on the sage inside to realign off-kilter situations.

Family Dynamics

If you have arguments at home, the next assignment provides a way to iron out constant family disputes. This exercise is a family meeting that uses a moderator. The moderator monitors the amount of time each person has to answer each question listed in the questionnaire. These questions are geared to exploring one's feelings about family dynamics. The moderator prohibits interruptions from others. The moderator explains that there is no right or wrong answer. The objective is to give each person a chance to express his or her feelings. The meeting progresses from young to old to avoid dominance of elders. There is a four-minute time limit for each question so the meeting moves along in a reasonable timeframe.

Δ **Exercise 26: Family Dynamics** (page 145)

Sometimes we are better able to participate with problem solving recommendations when there is little risk of having your commentary upset others. This family questionnaire essentially opens the door for free flowing communication, where trepidation is removed. You have the liberty to communicate freely without interruption or correction from others! Let your wildest ambitions be put into motion by having this family meeting while everyone is sharing a vacation.

Travel

My last trip to Europe is represented with lovely photos in this book. I was seriously depleted of funds during this vacation, but it was an impromptu decision. My niece and I went on this journey together with the expectation that my uncle had an apartment for the month. Instead he gave us an automobile and apologized that the apartment was rented. We only had fourteen hundred dollars for a five-week vacation, because we purchased an unlimited train pass that we unfortunately did not need. We were lucky to be in a country where it is legal to park overnight in a public lot to sleep in the vehicle. Additionally, we found public showers at camping sites. This unforgettable experience was a blessing, even though I felt like a vagabond. The companionship forged with my niece was fortified with jokes, songs and many insightful conversations. We discussed the past and present-day, because I was in Berlin twenty years earlier. We visited the plot of land where my mother once flocked and skipped along the crops that now have tremendous wind powered structures. This was the first time I retraced my mother's footsteps. This allowed us to discuss the origin of our heritage and the progression of life from a political and environmental standpoint. Here's one description of this wonderful travel experience:

In 1984, Berlin was quite a different town. The Iron Curtain divided the city into two distinct economies. The Berlin wall attempted to shield capitalism from communism, and this separation was fortified with land mines and militant guards. Manufacturing seemed to produce few products for the population. It felt like I was in a time warp from the 1940's as black and white movie would transform the color of real-life—everyone was wearing gray trench coats, thick-soled shoes and blah garments and underground subways were ghostly vacant. Billboards had government propaganda about the fair distribution of wealth and social values. The city was very clean. I met a young man who discussed social equality. He didn't object to restricted travel outside of his native country. He had many good things to say about communism. The availability of goods was obviously scarce and buildings were scared with bullet holes. On the capitalistic side of Berlin, there were modern updates and graffiti polluting the environment. Police, crime and vandalism were on display, but this changed after twenty years passed. Germany united into one nation from west to east in 1989, only five years later.

In 2004, I had the opportunity to roller blade through the streets of Berlin. This mode of transportation was possible because 9,000 people skate from late afternoon to eleven o'clock on a Thursday afternoon. It's called "Blade Night." The roads are closed for this event. This allowed me to see, feel and touch a whole new perspective. I felt the essence of happiness as wind passed through my hair, giving me an astounding sense of glee. The emotions were felt when I stood in the village that my mother enjoyed as a child. This cultural spanned further back than twenty years and for a short moment I was compelled to cry. I experienced a sense of sixty decades where the odds of survival were slim. I touched the ground of ancestors and I felt blessed.

A positive attitude is linked to that indispensable feeling that one is aware of their pleasures in life. Travel plays a vital role in developing a sense of adaptively and it exposes a person to music, art and sports. Travel is an introspective way of seeing the lives of others and appreciating modern-day conveniences. Travel includes some luxury, but usually it is a situation of making some compromise as well. When one returns from a vacation there is a renewal of self identity. This can spark the feelings that are outlined in the survey provided.

Δ Exercise 27: Self Identity (page 146)

Don't Worry

Worry is an instinct to prevent danger. We prepare for natural disaster by protecting our property and boarding windows when a storm approaches. We conduct a fire drill so we know what to do in case of an emergency. If you fear poverty, then you work hard to avoid this possibility. You save money to avoid overcome potential setbacks. If you fear a deficiency in intellect, you get a formal education to certify your abilities. Fear creates discipline. Ironically fear can be immobilizing as well. Rhonda Britten wrote a book called *Fearless Living*. This teaches readers to release fear, worry and anxiety with gratitude statements. Below is a list of gratitude statements that can resolve worrisome emotions. These statements are used to reframe a negative perspective into a positive attitude:

- How can I turn a recent disappointment into a positive statement?

- When I growl at a situation (the phone interrupts you), what statement will bring a different response? (Stating I'm glad people want to call me?)

- When I witnessed entertainment recently, how did I respond to this experience? (Did I judge the situation or did I show genuine appreciation.)

- How does fear influence my future?

- What is the risk of the potential fear?

Gratitude statements shift a focus away from a grouchy reaction. Gratitude statements should encourage an appreciation for personal safety, relationships and confidence. Here are gratitude statements I've used in the past month:

- I am glad my mother acknowledges me several times a week.

- I am glad for peaceful moments.

- I am happy to be able to help others.

- I am glad that am still learning new things.

- I am glad I have some wealth.

- I am glad that I do not blame others.

- I have a beautiful life.

- I was given a good education.

- I have a powerful faith in the universe.

- I have reliable tools.

- My body, mind and soul are rejuvenated.

We talked about the Cinderella Syndrome, which stems from the fairytale where a frumpy representation of tattered clothes, dirty knees and cracked fingernails were magically transformed. This was in the midst of a cruel stepmother ridiculing her in a painstaking effort to make life difficult. Cinderella had to "consider the source." Her fantasy for a handsome prince was blessed with wishful thinking. The power of passion intervened and she sung songs to boldly combat her potential. She had courage to smile brilliantly, even though life was smitten with mental abuse. When she was given opportunity, she was in the right place, with the right tools to use her special gifts. Standing in front of the King's palace, she presented a new image and curtsied with ease. Gracing her presence with good manners, she stepped across the ballroom floor on crystal pedestals and she was support in the arms of a gallivant prince who believed she was a miracle. Swept away in the moment, her time clock ticked like a bomb ready to explode. Alas, the prince couldn't reshape her life, until she did this first. But, love is relentless. This fairytale reaches a happily ever after conclusion to prove that human compassion prevails. It is an excellent example of self actualization.

Self Actualization

The pinnacle of success is not a case of perfection or abundant material possession. Success is a deep sense of purpose. Success is ambitiously oriented to helping others succeed. Self actualization taps into a higher consciousness of attracting good things with these principles:

1. Experience life selflessly.

2. Make a conscious choice between safety and risk.

3. Be accountable for your actions.

4. Develop skills that empower life.

5. Lose the illusion that you are a failure.

6. Learn what you are good at doing.

7. Discover who you are, what you like and what you don't like.

8. Determine what will hurt you and avoid those things.

9. Acknowledge fears as a way to overcome a concern.

Self actualization comes after many life transformations. It defines what you want, using a palette of experiences to guide decisions. Abraham Maslow, a famous psychologist during this past century, crafted this principle. He believed that self actualization is vital for happiness. Success is being able to creatively express oneself, without fear of condemnation by self or others. Success is dependent on an inner voice that has core principles. In a faction of a second, instant gratification can arrive. After looking at the quintessential mix of science and human emotion, we've bridged concepts of philosophy and psychology into twenty-eight experiments that conclude with the following self actualization survey, which will determine how a fraction of a second is used to create powerful choices in your life.

Δ Exercise 28: Self Actualization (page 147)

You have an opportunity to create intellectual property. You are able to broaden the scope of prosperity. You are privy to secrets of self or others, but integrity is understood. Good Samaritans know their special gifts will be to educate, lead, care for someone or inspire people to build things, heal wounds and spiritually enlighten another. The essence of compassion is the theme that restores hope for all communities and world religions.

Compassion

Coping is a learned skill. That was my thought while standing in front of the United Nations headquarters building—where a three-legged chair represents the difficulty of staying balanced when all nations attempt to work together on a common good. Humans are wealthy, wise and compassionate. Goodwill is at the mercy of wealth. Teamwork needs wisdom. Nations need compassion. Your sense of duty will fall into one of these qualities. Additionally, the nature of compassion must follow these conditions:

1. Love yourself as much as you love others.

2. Trust your gut instincts.

3. Don't confuse instant gratification with long-term happiness.

4. Recognize your achievements.

5. Seek support when you feel vulnerable.

6. Assess life transformational goals.

7. Negotiate with patience.

7. Negotiate with patience.

This journey looks at life transformation as a positive outcome. This process will reinforce virtues and mindful fundamentals that guide the soul with goals. Your creative outlets are able to work in process and these are in concert with self actualization principles. Special gifts offer a natural propensity for you to achieve mammoth results. You've learned to negotiate with less interference, even when it may appear that **"the man who has the gold can make or break the rules."** This is an expression I heard in Guyana, a country that is faced with a phenomenal amount of pressure to sell the rainforest to private investors. The destruction of a rainforest will benefit a few wealthy citizens in a third-world society that has an abundance of untapped resources. Rampant exploitation, urban sprawling and dense populations may lead to an inconvenient truth. There is hope to preserve the animal kingdom and our natural habitat, because the voice of an ordinary citizen can be heard. It is our civic duty to instill faith in our country's ability to foster responsiveness, fairness and righteousness. Recognize that the simple pleasures in life are unplugged. Believe in your potential. Be virtuous. Enjoy the most precious gift ever given—the choice to be passionate.

Liberty for All

Set your sights high for grand achievement

Challenges might expect bereavement

Evaluate results you hope to receive

Imagine what you want to believe

For your human responsibility

Is to defend the right for liberty.

Life with a Passion Appendix

Life Empowerment Makeover®

InsiteRose Publishing
PO Box 23843
Portland, OR 97281
503-624-7282

Please visit our website www.lifewithapassion.com for more information.

Thank you.

Family Credo

Our journey starts with a cultural portrait, which is a story of your heritage. This story focuses on key events, such as moving to a new home, experiencing a change in school, getting a job, etc. The objective is to clarify values. We conclude with this question, "Based on your life experiences, what resonates as your favorite slogan that you live by." or "What is the most valuable lesson you've learned in life?" Scribe this personal credo (mission statement) for each person here:

Father's Mission Statement:

....

....

....

....

....

Mother's Mission Statement:

....

....

....

....

....

Your Mission Statement:

....

....

....

....

....

Disposition Quiz

	Passive		
	No	Maybe	Yes
1. Do you communicate openly?			
2. Do you volunteer willingly in group activities?			
3. Do you avoid someone who is in a bad mood?			
4. Are you curious when someone is happy or angry?			
5. Do you usually ask for assistance?			
6. When attending a class, do you ask questions?			
7. When you first meet someone, is it easy to strike up a conversation?			
8. Do you reveal your feelings and beliefs easily?			
	No	Maybe	Yes
	Communicative		

	Assertive		
	No	Maybe	Yes
9. Do you press your side of an argument?			
10. Are you inclined to negotiate for a better price?			
11. Do you get impatient when waiting in a long line?			
12. Do you usually want to know why there is a delay?			
13. Do you believe fortune will be in your destiny?			
14. Do you allocate household chores to others?			
15. Are you apprehensive to ask for directions?			
16. Do you bend the rules to fit your needs?			
17. Do you usually guard your point of view?			
18. Are you inclined to attempt daring feats?			
19. Do you readily tell others about your opinions?			
	No	Maybe	Yes
	Aggressive		

	Pragmatic		
	No	Maybe	Yes
20. Do you enjoy doing craft projects?			
21. Are you a perfectionist with your work?			
22. Are you constantly thinking of imaginative ideas?			
23. Are you a workaholic?			
24. Are you eccentric?			
25. Do you often daydream about things to make?			

	No	Maybe	Yes
26. Do you collect things that might be useful later?			
27. Do you like to solve complicated problems?			
28. Do you frequently reward yourself?			
29. Do you often give gifts to friends or family?			
30. Do you do projects that take a long time to complete?			
	No	Maybe	Yes
			Creative

Introvert			
	No	Maybe	Yes
31. Do you feel you have a charming personality?			
32. Is your appearance always at its best?			
33. Do you eagerly reach out to shake hands?			
34. Do you like being at the center of attention?			
35. Do you look forward to social interactions?			
36. Do you dress with flamboyant colors?			
37. Do you prefer a social gathering to a quiet setting?			
38. Do you like the idea of being famous or popular?			
	No	Maybe	Yes
			Extrovert

Disciplined			
	No	Maybe	Yes
39. Are you bored on weekends?			
40. Do you enjoy new fashion trends?			
41. Are your vacations open-ended?			
42. Do you resist following suggestions made by others?			
43. Are you a bit unreliable at paying bills on time?			
44. Do you spend ample time relaxing on vacations?			
45. Do you feel unorganized much of the time?			
46. Do you avoid ironing clothes?			
47. Do you prefer impromptu activities?			
48. Do you try to avoid controlled environments?			
49. Do you like spontaneous activities?			
50. Do you prefer to not schedule too many events?			
	No	Maybe	Yes
			Unstructured

The Public Eye Chart

"Am I ___?"	Mother	Father	Sibling	Sibling	Friend	Friend	Self
Agreeable							
Controlling							
Defensive							
Detailed Oriented							
Distracted							
Discontent							
Easy Going							
Family Oriented							
Forgiving							
Funny/Humorous							
Goal oriented							
Grumpy							
Hardworking							
Health Conscious							
Honest							
Insulting							
Judgmental							
Loving							
On Time							
Modest/Humble							
Open minded							
Opportunity Seeking							
Organized							
Physically Active							
Resentful							
Resourceful							
Self-Defeating							
Shy							
Spiritual							
Talkative							
Willing to Help							
Well Mannered							

Ranking Scale: 0=never   1=seldom   2=occasionally   3=mostly   4=always

Self Awareness

1. What are my favorite character traits?

   ....

   ....

2. What traits do people see in me that I don't often think about?

   ....

   ....

3. What talents do I want to develop later in life?

   ....

   ....

4. What are my favorite brainstorming ideas?

   ....

   ....

5. What habits do I conceal from others?

   ....

   ....

6. What are the most commonly recognized skills I have to offer?

   ....

   ....

7. What recreational activities do I enjoy?

   ....

   ....

8. What are my key roles in life? (Parent, sibling, student)......................

....

9. How would I describe my best friends' virtues?

....

....

10. What careers would I like to investigate further?

....

....

11. I wish I felt better about...

at home ....

at work..

at school...

on vacation ....

12. Who are the most humorous people I enjoy seeing?

....

....

13. How can I increase exposure to people I really enjoy?

....

....

14. I feel intrigued by the success of these mentors, because...

....

....

Divorce Story

Divorce has a profound impact on most people. Usually there is an important lesson learned. The information below will assess how divorce has impacted your life, or someone you know dearly.

Who is divorced in my family?

....

....

....

What was the reason for these divorces (describe the story)?

....

....

....

....

....

How has divorce affected my life?

....

....

....

....

....

....

Anger Survey

1. When situations become disagreeable, this is my initial response: (Describe the Fight, Flight or Freeze response)

    ....

    ....

2. What is the most common reason for me to argue?

    ....

    ....

3. Who influences me to resolve arguments, and why?

    ....

    ....

4. Where do my arguments usually take place?

    ....

    ....

5. What skill should I develop so I'm less affected by an argument?

    ....

    ....

6. What are possible resolutions for a recent argument?

    ....

    ....

7. What is most likely to occur during arguments?

    ....

    ....

8. What is the outcome of most arguments I experience?

    ....

    ....

    ....

Love Survey

1. My definition of a loving connection is? ....
....
....

2. What was love like for my parents and/or grandparents?.....................
....
....

3. What do I expect from a loving relationship?....................................
....
....

4. What would be an extremely important wedding vow?.........................
....

5. My dream of a perfect mate would be described as: ....
....
....

6. These are the activities I want to share with a partner:.......................
....
....

7. It would be important to relinquish these responsibilities when I get
married:...
....

8. I would get married if:..
....
....

9. My partner would need to be considerate in these ways:.....................
....
....

Weekly Intentions®

ROLES (circle): *Aunt/Niece Brother Coworker Dad Daughter Grandparent Friend In-Law Mother Neighbor Sister Son Uncle/Nephew Other: _____*

GOALS (circle): *Athlete Artist Employee Gardener Musician Pet Owner*

I want to be especially nice to_____ this week.
I want to learn about _____ this week.
I want to do this _____ social activity this week.
I want to improve my health by doing _____ x____ this week.
I want to be involved in the world by _____ this week.

To-Dos *(tasks related to I Want intentions, check the box when you have done the activity.)*

- ☐ _____
- ☐ _____
- ☐ _____
- ☐ _____
- ☐ _____

Names of mentors:	Artistic-Creative	Athletic	Confident-Assured	Courageous	Dependable	Direct-Devoted	Energetic-Entertaining	Empowering-Inspirational	Friendly-Personable	Funny-Humorous	Generous-Charitable	Helpful-Conscientious	Honest-Honorable	Intelligent-World Wise	Humble-Peaceful	Meticulous-Organized	Successful	Tenacious-Hard Working	Well-spoken			

Habit Tracker®

	Mon	Tue	Wed	Thu	Fri	Sat	Sun
Meals	☐ ☐ ☐	☐ ☐ ☐	☐ ☐ ☐	☐ ☐ ☐	☐ ☐ ☐	☐ ☐ ☐	☐ ☐ ☐
Snacks	☐ ☐ ☐	☐ ☐ ☐	☐ ☐ ☐	☐ ☐ ☐	☐ ☐ ☐	☐ ☐ ☐	☐ ☐ ☐
Workouts	☐ ☐ ☐	☐ ☐ ☐	☐ ☐ ☐	☐ ☐ ☐	☐ ☐ ☐	☐ ☐ ☐	☐ ☐ ☐
Other	☐ ☐ ☐	☐ ☐ ☐	☐ ☐ ☐	☐ ☐ ☐	☐ ☐ ☐	☐ ☐ ☐	☐ ☐ ☐
	☐ ☐ ☐	☐ ☐ ☐	☐ ☐ ☐	☐ ☐ ☐	☐ ☐ ☐	☐ ☐ ☐	☐ ☐ ☐
	☐ ☐ ☐	☐ ☐ ☐	☐ ☐ ☐	☐ ☐ ☐	☐ ☐ ☐	☐ ☐ ☐	☐ ☐ ☐
	☐ ☐ ☐	☐ ☐ ☐	☐ ☐ ☐	☐ ☐ ☐	☐ ☐ ☐	☐ ☐ ☐	☐ ☐ ☐

DOME Journal

Record an argument or situation you want to resolve. Describe what happened—proceed with a journal describing the most recent occurrence where you have had a dispute.

Date: ....

Occurrence (describe the situation): ....
....
....
....
....
....

Who: ....
Where: ....

My Initial Response (Did I react with strong words or feelings?) How did I leave this situation?
....
....
....
....
....

Education Needed For Resolution: ....
....
....
....
....

What egos were revealed: ☐ **Child-Ego**   ☐ **Parent-Ego**   ☐ **Adult-Ego**

Egos and Rackets

An ego is present when you assume authority to act a certain way. A racket is a hardship that justifies a need to gain power or to get sympathy. Egos and rackets are often valid excuses, but they can be a crutch or a disservice to relationships. Track the frequency of a sentence that implies a specific ego or racket, so you can see the frequency of a behavior pattern (in parentheses).

☐	☐	☐	☐	☐	I had to because... (Adult Ego)
☐	☐	☐	☐	☐	I've never been able to... (Anxiety)
☐	☐	☐	☐	☐	If he does this, I'll... (Barter)
☐	☐	☐	☐	☐	They made me... (Blame)
☐	☐	☐	☐	☐	I don't care... (Child Ego)
☐	☐	☐	☐	☐	Because he did... (Co-Dependence)
☐	☐	☐	☐	☐	They can't make me... (Conformity)
☐	☐	☐	☐	☐	They have... (Comparison)
☐	☐	☐	☐	☐	I did it because... (Defensive)
☐	☐	☐	☐	☐	I don't have enough... (Deficiency)
☐	☐	☐	☐	☐	That's just the way it is. (Denial)
☐	☐	☐	☐	☐	I deserve it more than... (Entitlement)
☐	☐	☐	☐	☐	I worry about... (Fear)
☐	☐	☐	☐	☐	Look at what they did... (Humiliation)
☐	☐	☐	☐	☐	This happened to me because... (Justify)
☐	☐	☐	☐	☐	I have to have it now. (Impulsiveness)
☐	☐	☐	☐	☐	I'm not going to because... (Irrational)
☐	☐	☐	☐	☐	I worked so hard and now... (Martyr)
☐	☐	☐	☐	☐	They are trying to... (Paranoid)
☐	☐	☐	☐	☐	You better or else... (Parent Ego)
☐	☐	☐	☐	☐	I remember when I could... (Past)
☐	☐	☐	☐	☐	I can't because... (Pity)
☐	☐	☐	☐	☐	I'll get to it later... (Postpone)
☐	☐	☐	☐	☐	I shouldn't have, but... (Rationalize)
☐	☐	☐	☐	☐	It doesn't matter... (Surrender)
☐	☐	☐	☐	☐	I'm not __ enough... (Self-Defeat)
☐	☐	☐	☐	☐	I want to but... (Vague)

Depression Survey

1. What can I do to switch negative thinking into a positive attitude?

    ....

    ....

2. Who would help me avoid chronic depression?....................................

    ....

    ....

3. How can I prevent situations that cause prolonged sadness?...............

    ....

    ....

4. How does my lifestyle contribute to depression tendencies? ....

    ....

    ....

5. What lifestyle changes would make me a happier person?.................

    ....

    ....

6. What mantras motivate me?...

    ....

7. What is the likely outcome of drug use?..

    ....

8. What rewarding activities would enrich my soul? ....

    ....

Financial Questionnaire

1. I have loaned money or lent personal items to: ....
   ....

2. I plan to have the following debts satisfied by...............................
   ....

3. This year I have learned this very important lesson regarding
   money issues:...
   ....

4. Do I currently have ample life, medical, dental, long-term disability
   insurance? ....

5. What repairs (car, home) are necessary at this time?....................
   ....

6. What charitable donations have I made this year? ....
   ....

7. What money concerns do I have at this time?................................

8. What assets are listed in my Living Will? ....
   ....

9. Do I need to return or repair something broken or borrowed? ....

10. Have I postponed medical or dental treatments? ....
    ....

11. What are some of the financial promises I've made that haven't
    been fulfilled?..

12. What is my budget for continuing education this year? ....

13. To earn money doing my favorite things, I would have these careers:...

....

14. My first means of earning money was by doing these things:..............

....

15. My parents showed me how to manage money in the following ways:...

....

16. These are my current accounting habits:.................................

....

17. The accounting disciplines I want to practice are:......................

....

18. My family was financially rich, middle class or poor? ....

19. My biggest fear about money is: ....

20. These are my favorite things to purchase: ....

....

21. I wish I had enough money for:...

....

22. If I were rich, I'd...

....

23. The largest sum of money I have received at any one time was:........

24. This is what I did with that money: ....

Finance Tracker® - Paycheck Planning

Paycheck Dates:					
Income Amounts:					
40%-Necessity					
Child Care					
Food					
Electricity					
Garbage					
House payment					
Natural Gas					
Phone					
Taxes					
Water/Sewer					
20%-Social					
Cell Phone					
Charity/Tithing					
Dining Out					
Entertainment					
Movies					
Transportation					
20%-Luxury					
Car Insurance					
Car Payment					
Clothing					
Credit Cards					
Past Debts					
Bank Loans					
Vacations					
20%-Saving					
Automatic					
Emergency Fund					
Investments					
Remaining Balance	$	$	$	$	$

Monthly Finance Tracker®

40% NECESSITY Rent, Food, Taxes, Phone, Utilities	20%-SOCIAL Dining, Gasoline, Hobbies, Classes, Entertainment, Taxi	20%-LUXURY Boat, Car, Clothing, Credit Card Debt, Loans, Furnishings, Vacations.	20%-$NVESTMENTS Education, 401K, Stocks, Bonds
$	$	$	$
Income descriptions:			

Total all categories *(In=Income, N=Necessity, S=Social, L=Luxury, $=Savings)* from Finance Tracker® weekly records. Compare the percentages with the Ideal Spending Pyramid (40/20/20/20). Extrapolate those numbers for quarterly plans.

Quarterly Finance Tracker

Projected Income	Q1-Q2	Q3-Q4	Q1-Q2	Q3-Q4	Q1-Q2
Income Amounts:					
40%-Necessity					
Household Cost					
Property Taxes					
Child Care					
Income Taxes					
20%-Social					
Total:					
20%-Luxury					
Car Costs					
Clothing					
Debts					
Luxury Purchases					
Vacation					
Other:					
20%-Saving					
Education					
Other:					
Remaining Balance	$	$	$	$	$

Do I feel prepared for the next year, if so why? ....

What are my financial needs and wants this year? ....

Life Tracker® Weekly Finance Log

Payee	Circle Type*	Cash	Check	Credit
Sunday	Beg. Balance:			
	In N S L $			
	In N S L $			
	In N S L $			
	In N S L $			
	Balance:			
Monday	In N S L $			
	In N S L $			
	In N S L $			
	In N S L $			
	Balance:			
Tuesday	In N S L $			
	In N S L $			
	In N S L $			
	In N S L $			
	Balance:			
Wednesday	In N S L $			
	In N S L $			
	In N S L $			
	In N S L $			
	Balance:			
Thursday	In N S L $			
	In N S L $			
	In N S L $			
	In N S L $			
	Balance:			
Friday	In N S L $			
	In N S L $			
	In N S L $			
	In N S L $			
	Balance:			
Saturday	In N S L $			
	In N S L $			
	In N S L $			
	In N S L $			
	In N S L $			
* In=Income, N=Necessity, S= Social, L=Luxury, $=Savings/Investments	End Balance:			

Passionate Living: Month of _____

Goal this Month: _____

   Purpose _____

   Actions _____

   Rewards _____

   Timeline _____

   Special Resources _____

Suggestions / Feedback: _____

_____

_____

Inspirational Words, Quotes, Books or Movies: _____

_____

_____

Desirable Habits: _____

_____

_____

Important Decision

Pros	**Cons**
_____	_____
_____	_____
_____	_____
_____	_____
_____	_____
_____	_____

The above components are incorporated into Life Tracker's monthly calendars.

Life Tracker®

Mentor: _____

Gratitude:_____

Month & Day	Appt Time
Monday	
Tuesday	

Life Tracker®

Mentor: _____

Gratitude: _____

Month & Day	Appt Time
Wednesday	
Thursday	

Life Tracker®

Mentor: _____

Gratitude:_____

Month & Day	Appt Time
Friday	

Saturday	Sunday

Personal Billboard

KEEP HOUSE CLEAN daily

Supportive
Opportunist
Neat
Jolly
Appreciate

- a mentor for kids
- $250,000 in 15 years
- creative outlets
- a trustworthy person
- a worldly person
- intelligent
- on-time
- caring

**B
I
K
E**

**G
O
L
F**

**H
I
K
E**

weekly

LIFE WITH
A PASSION

YOGA or
DANCE

ROMANCE monthly

Photographs were clipped from magazines to represent goals. These photographs are of unknown origin. They were used for my personal billboard. The original format size is 2'x2'. These pictures represent places to visit and words related to my goals.

Family Dynamics

A moderator reads each question below for a family member. This moderator will summarize the meeting and monitor the time spent for each question. Each person gets four minutes to answer each question or to offer feedback. He or she will answer all questions before other members provide feedback. Start with the youngest person, and move along to the next oldest person. If a child is rather young, just have him or her answer the first five questions. No one is allowed to interrupt the person speaking. Dialogue is open for feedback in rotation of youngest to oldest. Here are the questions:

1. What type of future do you foresee for each person in your family two years from now?

2. What would you rather visualize for each person's future?

3. If you could have one rule established in the family, what would it be? (For example: I would like no more yelling.)

4. What bad habits occur during arguments?

5. Explain a recent problem in the family. What troubled you the most about this situation?

6. Do you feel unreasonable expectations are placed upon you, if so, what are the demands that frustrate you?

7. What do you expect from others in the family?

8. Is fair distribution of chores for each person in the family?

9. Do you feel there is a nutritional balance in family meals?

10. What are your recommendations for punishment policies?

11. How can you reduce the stress that exists in the family?

12. How can you help others achieve their goals?

13. What would you like to experience on family vacations?

14. What is the top goal derived from answering these questions?

Self-Identity

One can reach the height of personal success by realizing the nature of self–identity. The following questions clarify a positive outlook:

1. What three wishes would you hope for, if anything were possible?

2. Who is your key mentor and why is this person such an inspiration for you?

3. If you were given a billion dollars, what would you do with that money?

4. What advice would you give to the citizens of this country?

5. Who is the best support person in your life?

6. What were your greatest achievements in the past year?

7. Who became a good friend during the past year?

8. Who did you help during the past year?

9. What was your most thrilling adventure?

10. What did you learn last year that you would do differently in the pending year to come?

Self-Actualization

1. List your favorite virtues and proverbs.

2. How will you reinforce Personal Time Off?

3. What do you do to express kindness for others?

4. How do you define long-term happiness?

5. Who relies on your encouragement?

6. What hostile environments or vindictive people will you avoid?

7. What rewards are you considering for the future?

8. What style of music affirms gratitude in your life?

9. Who provides an open-minded willingness to understand your perspective?

10. How can you negotiate with greater patience?

11. What are your key goals for the next three years?

12. What are your special gifts?

☐ To educate people

☐ To lead others

☐ To entertain others

☐ To care for someone in need

☐ To inspire others to achieve their very best

☐ To build things

☐ To heal the public

☐ To connect others with a spiritual mission

☐ To support others

Empowerment Notes

in
Site
Rose
Publishing

Life with a Passion
ORDER FORM

Name _____

Address _____   M/C   Visa

City & State _____   ☐   ☐

Zip code _____ Card # _____

Telephone _____ Expire Date:

Email _____ | Email-OK? ☐

Please use the billing address for your credit card here: | Check Enclosed? ☐

Qty	Product	Price	Total
	Life with a Passion, a softbound book	$14.95	
	Life Tracker, a semi-annual dated planner:	$14.95	
	Circle Start Date: Jan-June or July-Dec		
	Organizational Journal & Weekly Intentions	$12.95	
	Finance Tracker, annual budgets	$12.95	
	Life Jacket, a book wallet	$19.95	
	Life Empowerment Makeover, workshop materials	$ 3.95	
	Life Empowerment Workshop, per person or family	$35.00	
	(Sales tax is not necessary) Sub-Total		
	Shipping: $4.05 per order (see exemptions*) Shipping		
	All prices are stated in US dollars and are subject to change without notice. Grand Total:		

Workshop

Date: _____ Time: _____

Location: _____

Needs: _____

| * No shipping costs for workshops or if three+ items are ordered. | Credit Card Signature: |

InsiteRose Publishing
PO Box 23843
Portland, Oregon 97281

Initial here to authorize a semi-annual Life Tracker subscription: _____

Life with a Passion.. $14.95

This paperback book is an unforgettable exploration to enrich relationships. It provides a set of exercises to clarify your goals, evaluate courage and a to develop a positive attitude. There are short stories interspersed about the author's life empowerment journey of discovery.

Life Tracker° $14.95

This planner records activities for time and money. Contact pages and monthly calendars are in the front. Weekly pages include a finance log. This planner has ample writing space using a semi-annual approach. It has a durable plastic coil and a sturdy laminated cover.

Organizational Journal° $12.95

This booklet retains valuable information that comes to you in a random way. You get 52 lined pages that with alphabetical tabs to note important content related to the index (such as books to read, medical records, favorite movies, quotes, etc). This journal includes Weekly Intentions°.

Finance Tracker° $12.95

This system tracks annual budgets and accounts to track child support, credit accounts, tax expenses, etc. It provides a vertical orientation for cash-check-credit and debit activities for a lot of monetary transactions.

Life Jacket° $19.95

This book wallet has a beautiful silkscreen image of an eagle looking at the globe and rock climber. It holds Life Tracker, the Organizational Journal and Finance Tracker together with pockets for cash, credit cards and photos. It has a handy pen holster as well.

Life Empowerment Makeover°....................... $ 3.95

This is a reprint of the Life with a Passion Appendix.

Bibliography

Back, Ken and Kate. *Assertiveness at Work.* London: McGraw-Hill Book Co., 1982

Bassett, Lucinda. *Life Without Limits.* New York: Harper Collins, 2001

Branden, Nathaniel. *The Art of Living Consciously,* The Power of Awareness to Transform Everyday Life. New York, NY: Simon & Schuster, 1997

Britten, Rhonda. *Fearless Living,* Life Without Excuses and Love Without Regrets. New York, NY: Penguin Putnam, 2001

Bolton, Robert, Ph.D. *People Skills:* How to Assert Yourself, Listen to Others, and Resolve Conflict. New York, NY: Simon & Schuster, 1979

Borg, Marcus J. *Meeting Jesus Again for the First Time,* The Historical Jesus & The Heart of Contemporary. New York: Harper Collins Publishers, 1994

Bruer, John T., M.D. *The Myth of the First Three Years.* A New Understanding of Early Brain Development and Lifelong Learning. New York, NY: Simon & Schuster, 1999.

Burns, David D., MD. *Feeling Good.* The New Mood Therapy. New York, NY: Avon Books, 1980

Buscaglia, Leo F., Ph.D. *Loving Each Other.* The Challenge of Human Relationships. New York, NY: Ballantine Books, 1984

Christensen, Bobbie & Eric. *Building Your Financial Portfolio on $25 a Month.* Sacramento, CA: Effective Living Publishing, 2003

Chopra, Deepak. *The Seven Spiritual Laws of Success,* A Practical Guide to the Fulfillment of Your Dreams. San Rafael, CA: Amber-Allen Publishing, 1994

Covey, Sean. *The 7 Habits of Highly Effective Teens.* New York, NY: Simon & Schuster, 1998

DeAngelis, Barbara, Ph.D. *Are You The One For Me?* Knowing Who's Right & Avoiding Who's Wrong. New York, NY: Dell Publishing, 1992

Fassler, David G., M.D. and Lynne S. Dumas. *Help Me, I'm Sad,* Recognizing, Treating and Preventing Childhood and Adolescent Depression. New York, NY: Penguin Books, 1997

Fromm, Erich. *The Art of Loving.* New York, NY: Harper & Row Publishers, 1956

Geller, Anne, M.D. with Territo, M. J. *Restore Your Life,* a Living Plan for Sober People. New York, NY: Bantan Books, a Philip Lief Group Book, 1991

Goldman, Daniel. *Emotional Intelligence.* New York, NY: Bantam Books, 1994

Greist, John H. and James W. Jefferson, M.D. *Depression and Its Treatment.* Washington DC, Warner Books, 1992

Hill, Napoleon. *Keys to Success,* The 17 Principles of Personal Achievement. Middlesex, England, Penguin Books, 1997

Hunt, Mary. *Debt-Proof Living,* The Complete Guide to Living Financially Free. Nashville TN, Broadman & Holman Publishing, 1999

Jeffers, Susan, Ph. D. *Feel the Fear and Do It Anyway:* Dynamic Techniques for Turning Fear, Indecision and Anger into Power, Action and Love. New York, NY: Ballantine Books, 1987

Keen, Sam. *The Passionate Life,* Stages of Loving. New York, N: HarperCollins Publishers, 1983.

Kilpatrick, William. *Why Johnny Can't Tell from Right and Wrong: And What We Can Do About It.* New York, NY: Simon & Schuster Touchtone, 1992

Lama, Dalai and Culter, Howard, M.D. *The Art of Happiness, A Handbook for Living.* New York, NY: Riverhead Books, a member of Penguin Putnam Inc, 1998

Lakein, Alan. *How to Get Control of Your Time and Your Life.* New York, NY: David McKay Co., 1973

Leon, Cytryn, M.D and Donald McKnew, M.D. *Growing Up Sad, Childhood Depression and Its Treatment.* New York, NY: W.W. Norton, 1996

Lerner, Harriet G., Ph.D. *The Dance of Anger: A Woman's Guide to Changing the Patterns of Intimate Relationships.* New York, NY: Harper & Row Publishers, 1985

McKenna, Paul, Ph.D. *Change Your Life in 7 Days.* New York, NY: Harmony Books 2004

Menninger, Karl, M.D. *Whatever Became of Sin?* New York, NY: Hawthorn Books, 1973

Myers, Robert J. *What Everyone Should Know About Social Security.* Fairfax, VA: The Seniors Coalition, Inc. 1993

Morris, Kenneth M. & Alan M. Siegel. *Wall Street Journal, Guide to Understanding Personal Finance.* New York, NY Simon & Schuster Lightbulb Press, 1992

Nemeth, Maria, Ph.D. *The Energy of Money, a Spiritual Guide to Financial and Personal Fulfillment.* New York, NY: The Ballantine Publishing Group, 1999

Oldham, John M. M.D. & Lois B. Morris. *Personality Self-Portrait, Why You Think, Work, Love and Act the Way You Do.* New York, NY: Bantam Books, 1990.

Page, Susan. *If We're So in Love, Why Aren't We Happy?* New York, NY: Harmony Books, 2002

Peck, M. Scott, M.D. *The Road Less Traveled.* New York, NY: Simon & Schuster, 1978

Sachs, Jeffery D. *The End of Poverty, Economic Possibilities for Our Time.* New York, NY: Penguin Books, 2005

Strauss, Claudia J. **Talking to Depression**: Simple Ways to Connect When Someone in Your Life is Depressed. London, UK: Penguin Books, 2004

Strauss, Steven D. *Debt and Bankruptcy, Ask a Lawyer – Expert Advice That Will Save You Money.* New York, NY: W.W. Norton & Company, 1998

Tieger Paul D. & Barron-Tieger, Barbara. **Nurture by Nature.** *Understand Your Child's Personality Type—And Become a Better Parent.* Toronto, Canada: Little, Brown & Company Ltd, 1997

Twist, Lynne. *The Soul of Money, Transforming Your Relationship with Money and Life.* New York, NY: Warner Books, 1998

Von Oech, Roger. **A Whack on the Side of the Head.** How You Can Be More Creative. *New York, NY: Warner Books, 1998*

Whitfield, Charles L. **Healing the Child Within.** Discovery and Recovery for Adult Children of Dysfunctional Families. *Deerfield Beach, FL: Health Communications, 1987*

Life with a Passion Index

The Journey of Discovery

Has reached a conclusion.